Reflections

OCR (Oxford, Cambridge and RSA Examinations)
1 Hills Road, Cambridge, CB1 2EU

ISBN 978 019 9128020

Designed and produced by Oxford University Press

Cover image: Shutterstock

Printed in Great Britain by W. M. Print Ltd., Walsall

10 9 8 7 6 5 4 3

Introduction

Reflections is OCR's new collection of Heritage and Contemporary poems designed to meet the requirements of the National Curriculum Programme of Study and of the QCDA Subject Criteria for GCSE English, English Language and English Literature.

There are 15 poems for each poet and *Reflections* offers teachers and their students the opportunity to study their chosen poet in depth.

Using *Reflections* with the OCR specifications

Detailed information can be found in the OCR specifications and support materials.

J350 GCSE English

Unit A641: Reading Literary Texts

Wilfred Owen, Carol Ann Duffy and Benjamin Zephaniah are optional poetry choices for this unit.

J355 GCSE English Language

Unit A651: Extended Literary Text and Imaginative Writing

Wilfred Owen, Simon Armitage, Carol Ann Duffy and Benjamin Zephaniah are optional poetry choices for this unit.

J360 GCSE English Literature

Unit A661: Literary Heritage Linked Texts

Candidates are required to study **one** of the following poets:
Robert Browning, Geoffrey Chaucer, Thomas Hardy, Wilfred Owen, Christina Rossetti, William Shakespeare (Sonnets).

Unit A664: Literary Heritage Prose and Contemporary Poetry

Candidates are required to study **one** of the following poets:
Simon Armitage, Gillian Clarke, Wendy Cope, Carol Ann Duffy, Seamus Heaney, Benjamin Zephaniah.

Reflections could also be used as the basis to prepare students for the Unseen Poetry option.

Contents

Literary Heritage Poetry 9

Christina Rossetti

William Shakespeare

Contemporary Poetry

Carol Ann Duffy

Seamus Heaney

Benjamin Zephaniah

Literary Heritage Poetry

Robert Browning

Confessions

I

What is he buzzing in my ears?
  'Now that I come to die,
Do I view the world as a vale of tears?'
  Ah, reverend sir, not I!

II

5 What I viewed there once, what I view again
  Where the physic bottles stand
On the table's edge,—is a suburb lane,
  With a wall to my bedside hand.

III

That lane sloped, much as the bottles do,
10   From a house you could descry
O'er the garden-wall: is the curtain blue
  Or green to a healthy eye?

IV

To mine, it serves for the old June weather
  Blue above lane and wall;
15 And that farthest bottle labelled 'Ether'
  Is the house o'ertopping all.

V

At a terrace, somewhere near the stopper,
  There watched for me, one June,
A girl: I know, sir, it's improper,
20   My poor mind's out of tune.

VI

Only, there was a way . . . you crept
  Close by the side, to dodge
Eyes in the house, two eyes except:
  They styled their house 'The Lodge.'

VII

25 What right had a lounger up their lane?
  But, by creeping very close,
With the good wall's help,—their eyes might strain
  And stretch themselves to Oes,

VIII

Yet never catch her and me together,
30   As she left the attic, there,
By the rim of the bottle labelled 'Ether,'
  And stole from stair to stair,

IX

And stood by the rose-wreathed gate. Alas,
  We loved, sir—used to meet:
35 How sad and bad and mad it was—
  But then, how it was sweet!

Evelyn Hope

I

Beautiful Evelyn Hope is dead!
   Sit and watch by her side an hour.
That is her book-shelf, this her bed;
   She plucked that piece of geranium-flower,
5 Beginning to die too, in the glass;
   Little has yet been changed, I think:
The shutters are shut, no light may pass
   Save two long rays thro' the hinge's chink.

II

Sixteen years old when she died!
10   Perhaps she had scarcely heard my name;
It was not her time to love; beside,
   Her life had many a hope and aim,
Duties enough and little cares,
   And now was quiet, now astir,
15 Till God's hand beckoned unawares,—
   And the sweet white brow is all of her.

III

Is it too late then, Evelyn Hope?
   What, your soul was pure and true,
The good stars met in your horoscope,
20   Made you of spirit, fire and dew—
And, just because I was thrice as old
   And our paths in the world diverged so wide,
Each was nought to each, must I be told?
   We were fellow mortals, nought beside?

IV

25 No, indeed! for God above
   Is great to grant, as mighty to make,
And creates the love to reward the love:
   I claim you still, for my own love's sake!
Delayed it may be for more lives yet,
30   Through worlds I shall traverse, not a few:
Much is to learn, much to forget
   Ere the time be come for taking you.

V

But the time will come,—at last it will,
　　When, Evelyn Hope, what meant (I shall say)
35　In the lower earth, in the years long still,
　　That body and soul so pure and gay?
Why your hair was amber, I shall divine,
　　And your mouth of your own geranium's red—
And what you would do with me, in fine,
40　　In the new life come in the old one's stead.

VI

I have lived (I shall say) so much since then,
　　Given up myself so many times,
Gained me the gains of various men,
　　Ransacked the ages, spoiled the climes;
45　Yet one thing, one, in my soul's full scope,
　　Either I missed or itself missed me:
And I want and find you, Evelyn Hope!
　　What is the issue? let us see!

VII

I loved you, Evelyn, all the while.
50　　My heart seemed full as it could hold?
There was place and to spare for the frank young smile,
　　And the red young mouth, and the hair's young gold.
So, hush,—I will give you this leaf to keep:
　　See, I shut it inside the sweet cold hand!
55　There, that is our secret: go to sleep!
　　You will wake, and remember, and understand.

Home-Thoughts, from Abroad

I

Oh, to be in England
Now that April's there,
And whoever wakes in England
Sees, some morning, unaware,
5   That the lowest boughs and the brushwood sheaf
Round the elm-tree bole are in tiny leaf,
While the chaffinch sings on the orchard bough
In England – now!

II

And after April, when May follows,
10   And the whitethroat builds, and all the swallows!
Hark, where my blossomed pear-tree in the hedge
Leans to the field and scatters on the clover
Blossoms and dewdrops – at the bent spray's edge –
That's the wise thrush; he sings each song twice over,
15   Lest you should think he never could recapture
The first fine careless rapture!
And though the fields look rough with hoary dew,
All will be gay when noontide wakes anew
The buttercups, the little children's dower
20   – Far brighter than this gaudy melon-flower!

'How They Brought the Good News from Ghent to Aix'

[16—]

I

I sprang to the stirrup, and Joris, and he;
I galloped, Dirck galloped, we galloped all three;
'Good speed!' cried the watch, as the gate-bolts undrew;
'Speed!' echoed the wall to us galloping through;
5　Behind shut the postern, the lights sank to rest,
And into the midnight we galloped abreast.

II

Not a word to each other; we kept the great pace
Neck by neck, stride by stride, never changing our place;
I turned in my saddle and made its girths tight,
10　Then shortened each stirrup, and set the pique right,
Rebuckled the cheek-strap, chained slacker the bit,
Nor galloped less steadily Roland a whit.

III

'Twas moonset at starting; but while we drew near
Lokeren, the cocks crew and twilight dawned clear;
15　At Boom, a great yellow star came out to see;
At Düffeld, 'twas morning as plain as could be;
And from Mecheln church-steeple we heard the half-chime,
So, Joris broke silence with, 'Yet there is time!'

IV

At Aershot, up leaped of a sudden the sun,
20　And against him the cattle stood black every one,
To stare thro' the mist at us galloping past,
And I saw my stout galloper Roland at last,
With resolute shoulders, each butting away
The haze, as some bluff river headland its spray:

V

25　And his low head and crest, just one sharp ear bent back
For my voice, and the other pricked out on his track;
And one eye's black intelligence,—ever that glance
O'er its white edge at me, his own master, askance!
And the thick heavy spume-flakes which aye and anon
30　His fierce lips shook upwards in galloping on.

VI

By Hasselt, Dirck groaned; and cried Joris, 'Stay spur!
Your Roos galloped bravely, the fault's not in her,
We'll remember at Aix'—for one heard the quick wheeze
Of her chest, saw the stretched neck and staggering knees,
35 And sunk tail, and horrible heave of the flank,
As down on her haunches she shuddered and sank.

VII

So, we were left galloping, Joris and I,
Past Looz and past Tongres, no cloud in the sky;
The broad sun above laughed a pitiless laugh,
40 'Neath our feet broke the brittle bright stubble like chaff;
Till over by Dalhem a dome-spire sprang white,
And 'Gallop,' gasped Joris, 'for Aix is in sight!'

VIII

'How they'll greet us!'—and all in a moment his roan
Rolled neck and croup over, lay dead as a stone;
45 And there was my Roland to bear the whole weight
Of the news which alone could save Aix from her fate,
With his nostrils like pits full of blood to the brim,
And with circles of red for his eye-sockets' rim.

IX

Then I cast loose my buffcoat, each holster let fall,
50 Shook off both my jack-boots, let go belt and all,
Stood up in the stirrup, leaned, patted his ear,
Called my Roland his pet-name, my horse without peer;
Clapped my hands, laughed and sang, any noise, bad or good,
Till at length into Aix Roland galloped and stood.

X

55 And all I remember is—friends flocking round
As I sat with his head 'twixt my knees on the ground;
And no voice but was praising this Roland of mine,
As I poured down his throat our last measure of wine,
Which (the burgesses voted by common consent)
60 Was no more than his due who brought good news from Ghent.

James Lee's Wife
III – In the Doorway

I

The swallow has set her six young on the rail,
    And looks sea-ward:
The water's in stripes like a snake, olive-pale
    To the leeward, –
5 On the weather-side, black, spotted white with the wind.
'Good fortune departs, and disaster's behind,' –
Hark, the wind with its wants and its infinite wail!

II

Our fig-tree, that leaned for the saltness, has furled
    Her five fingers,
10 Each leaf like a hand opened wide to the world
    Where there lingers
No glint of the gold, Summer sent for her sake:
How the vines writhe in rows, each impaled on its stake!
My heart shrivels up and my spirit shrinks curled.

III

15 Yet here are we two; we have love, house enough,
    With the field there,
This house of four rooms, that field red and rough,
    Though it yield there,
For the rabbit that robs, scarce a blade or a bent;
20 If a magpie alight now, it seems an event;
And they both will be gone at November's rebuff.

IV

But why must cold spread? but wherefore bring change
    To the spirit,
God meant should mate his with an infinite range,
25   And inherit
His power to put life in the darkness and cold?
Oh, live and love worthily, bear and be bold!
Whom Summer made friends of, let Winter estrange!

Meeting at Night

I

The grey sea and the long black land;
And the yellow half-moon large and low;
And the startled little waves that leap
In fiery ringlets from their sleep,
5 As I gain the cove with pushing prow,
And quench its speed i' the slushy sand.

II

Then a mile of warm sea-scented beach;
Three fields to cross till a farm appears;
A tap at the pane, the quick sharp scratch
10 And blue spurt of a lighted match,
And a voice less loud, thro' its joys and fears,
Than the two hearts beating each to each!

Parting at Morning

Round the cape of a sudden came the sea,
And the sun looked over the mountain's rim:
And straight was a path of gold for him,
And the need of a world of men for me.

My Last Duchess

Ferrara

That's my last Duchess painted on the wall,
Looking as if she were alive. I call
That piece a wonder, now: Frà Pandolf's hands
Worked busily a day, and there she stands.
5 Will't please you sit and look at her? I said
'Frà Pandolf' by design, for never read
Strangers like you that pictured countenance,
The depth and passion of its earnest glance,
But to myself they turned (since none puts by
10 The curtain I have drawn for you, but I)
And seemed as they would ask me, if they durst,
How such a glance came there; so, not the first
Are you to turn and ask thus. Sir, 'twas not
Her husband's presence only, called that spot
15 Of joy into the Duchess' cheek: perhaps
Frà Pandolf chanced to say 'Her mantle laps
Over my lady's wrist too much,' or 'Paint
Must never hope to reproduce the faint
Half-flush that dies along her throat:' such stuff
20 Was courtesy, she thought, and cause enough
For calling up that spot of joy. She had
A heart—how shall I say?—too soon made glad,
Too easily impressed; she liked whate'er
She looked on, and her looks went everywhere.
25 Sir, 'twas all one! My favour at her breast,
The dropping of the daylight in the West,
The bough of cherries some officious fool
Broke in the orchard for her, the white mule
She rode with round the terrace—all and each
30 Would draw from her alike the approving speech,
Or blush, at least. She thanked men,—good! but thanked
Somehow—I know not how—as if she ranked
My gift of a nine-hundred-years-old name
With anybody's gift. Who'd stoop to blame

35 This sort of trifling? Even had you skill
    In speech—(which I have not)—to make your will
    Quite clear to such an one, and say, 'Just this
    Or that in you disgusts me; here you miss,
    Or there exceed the mark'—and if she let
40 Herself be lessoned so, nor plainly set
    Her wits to yours, forsooth, and made excuse,
    —E'en then would be some stooping; and I choose
    Never to stoop. Oh sir, she smiled, no doubt,
    Whene'er I passed her; but who passed without
45 Much the same smile? This grew; I gave commands;
    Then all smiles stopped together. There she stands
    As if alive. Will't please you rise? We'll meet
    The company below, then. I repeat,
    The Count your master's known munificence
50 Is ample warrant that no just pretence
    Of mine for dowry will be disallowed;
    Though his fair daughter's self, as I avowed
    At starting, is my object. Nay, we'll go
    Together down, sir. Notice Neptune, though,
55 Taming a sea-horse, thought a rarity,
    Which Claus of Innsbruck cast in bronze for me!

Never the Time and the Place

Never the time and the place
    And the loved one all together!
This path—how soft to pace!
    This May—what magic weather!
5 Where is the loved one's face?
In a dream that loved one's face meets mine,
    But the house is narrow, the place is bleak
Where, outside, rain and wind combine
    With a furtive ear, if I strive to speak,
10 With a hostile eye at my flushing cheek,
With a malice that marks each word, each sign!
O enemy sly and serpentine,
    Uncoil thee from the waking man!
      Do I hold the Past
15   Thus firm and fast
    Yet doubt if the Future hold I can?
This path so soft to pace shall lead
Thro' the magic of May to herself indeed!
Or narrow if needs the house must be,
20 Outside are the storms and strangers: we—
Oh, close, safe, warm sleep I and she,
    —I and she!

Now

Out of your whole life give but a moment!
All of your life that has gone before,
All to come after it, – so you ignore,
So you make perfect the present, – condense,
5 In a rapture of rage, for perfection's endowment,
Thought and feeling and soul and sense –
Merged in a moment which gives me at last
You around me for once, you beneath me, above me –
Me – sure that despite of time future, time past, –
10 This tick of our life-time's one moment you love me!
How long such suspension may linger? Ah, Sweet –
The moment eternal – just that and no more –
When ecstasy's utmost we clutch at the core
While cheeks burn, arms open, eyes shut and lips meet!

Porphyria's Lover

The rain set early in to-night,
    The sullen wind was soon awake,
It tore the elm-tops down for spite,
    And did its worst to vex the lake:
5   I listened with heart fit to break.
When glided in Porphyria; straight
    She shut the cold out and the storm,
And kneeled and made the cheerless grate
    Blaze up, and all the cottage warm;
10   Which done, she rose, and from her form
Withdrew the dripping cloak and shawl,
    And laid her soiled gloves by, untied
Her hat and let the damp hair fall,
    And, last, she sat down by my side
15   And called me. When no voice replied,
She put my arm about her waist,
    And made her smooth white shoulder bare,
And all her yellow hair displaced,
    And, stooping, made my cheek lie there,
20   And spread, o'er all, her yellow hair,
Murmuring how she loved me—she
    Too weak, for all her heart's endeavour,
To set its struggling passion free
    From pride, and vainer ties dissever,
25   And give herself to me for ever.
But passion sometimes would prevail,
    Nor could to-night's gay feast restrain
A sudden thought of one so pale
    For love of her, and all in vain:
30   So, she was come through wind and rain.

Be sure I looked up at her eyes
    Happy and proud; at last I knew
Porphyria worshipped me; surprise
    Made my heart swell, and still it grew
35   While I debated what to do.
That moment she was mine, mine, fair,
    Perfectly pure and good: I found
A thing to do, and all her hair
    In one long yellow string I wound
40   Three times her little throat around,
And strangled her. No pain felt she;
    I am quite sure she felt no pain.
As a shut bud that holds a bee,
    I warily oped her lids: again
45   Laughed the blue eyes without a stain.
And I untightened next the tress
    About her neck; her cheek once more
Blushed bright beneath my burning kiss:
    I propped her head up as before,
50   Only, this time my shoulder bore
Her head, which droops upon it still:
    The smiling rosy little head,
So glad it has its utmost will,
    That all it scorned at once is fled,
55   And I, its love, am gained instead!
Porphyria's love: she guessed not how
    Her darling one wish would be heard.
And thus we sit together now,
    And all night long we have not stirred,
60   And yet God has not said a word!

The Laboratory

Ancien Régime

I

Now that I, tying thy glass mask tightly,
May gaze thro' these faint smokes curling whitely,
As thou pliest thy trade in this devil's-smithy—
Which is the poison to poison her, prithee?

II

5 He is with her, and they know that I know
Where they are, what they do: they believe my tears flow
While they laugh, laugh at me, at me fled to the drear
Empty church, to pray God in, for them!—I am here.

III

Grind away, moisten and mash up thy paste,
10 Pound at thy powder,—I am not in haste!
Better sit thus, and observe thy strange things,
Than go where men wait me and dance at the King's.

IV

That in the mortar—you call it a gum?
Ah, the brave tree whence such gold oozings come!
15 And yonder soft phial, the exquisite blue,
Sure to taste sweetly,—is that poison too?

V

Had I but all of them, thee and thy treasures,
What a wild crowd of invisible pleasures!
To carry pure death in an earring, a casket,
20 A signet, a fan-mount, a filigree basket!

VI

Soon, at the King's, a mere lozenge to give,
And Pauline should have just thirty minutes to live!
But to light a pastile, and Elise, with her head
And her breast and her arms and her hands, should drop dead!

VII

25 Quick—is it finished? The colour's too grim!
Why not soft like the phial's, enticing and dim?
Let it brighten her drink, let her turn it and stir,
And try it and taste, ere she fix and prefer!

VIII

What a drop! She's not little, no minion like me!
30 That's why she ensnared him: this never will free
The soul from those masculine eyes,—say, 'no!'
To that pulse's magnificent come-and-go.

IX

For only last night, as they whispered, I brought
My own eyes to bear on her so, that I thought
35 Could I keep them one half minute fixed, she would fall
Shrivelled; she fell not; yet this does it all!

X

Not that I bid you spare her the pain;
Let death be felt and the proof remain:
Brand, burn up, bite into its grace—
40 He is sure to remember her dying face!

XI

Is it done? Take my mask off! Nay, be not morose;
It kills her, and this prevents seeing it close:
The delicate droplet, my whole fortune's fee!
If it hurts her, beside, can it ever hurt me?

XII

45 Now, take all my jewels, gorge gold to your fill,
You may kiss me, old man, on my mouth if you will!
But brush this dust off me, lest horror it brings
Ere I know it—next moment I dance at the King's!

The Last Ride Together

I

I said—Then, dearest, since 't is so,
Since now at length my fate I know,
Since nothing all my love avails,
Since all, my life seemed meant for, fails,
5   Since this was written and needs must be—
My whole heart rises up to bless
Your name in pride and thankfulness!
Take back the hope you gave,—I claim
Only a memory of the same,
10 —And this beside, if you will not blame,
    Your leave for one more last ride with me.

II

My mistress bent that brow of hers;
Those deep dark eyes where pride demurs
When pity would be softening through,
15 Fixed me a breathing-while or two
    With life or death in the balance: right!
The blood replenished me again;
My last thought was at least not vain:
I and my mistress, side by side
20 Shall be together, breathe and ride,
So, one day more am I deified.
    Who knows but the world may end to-night?

III

Hush! if you saw some western cloud
All billowy-bosomed, over-bowed
25 By many benedictions—sun's
And moon's and evening-star's at once—
    And so, you, looking and loving best,
Conscious grew, your passion drew
Cloud, sunset, moonrise, star-shine too,
30 Down on you, near and yet more near,
Till flesh must fade for heaven was here!—
Thus leant she and lingered—joy and fear!
    Thus lay she a moment on my breast.

IV

Then we began to ride. My soul
35 Smoothed itself out, a long-cramped scroll
Freshening and fluttering in the wind.
Past hopes already lay behind.
    What need to strive with a life awry?
Had I said that, had I done this,
40 So might I gain, so might I miss.
Might she have loved me? just as well
She might have hated, who can tell!
Where had I been now if the worst befell?
    And here we are riding, she and I.

V

45 Fail I alone, in words and deeds?
Why, all men strive and who succeeds?
We rode; it seemed my spirit flew,
Saw other regions, cities new,
    As the world rushed by on either side.
50 I thought,—All labour, yet no less
Bear up beneath their unsuccess.
Look at the end of work, contrast
The petty done, the undone vast,
This present of theirs with the hopeful past!
55   I hoped she would love me; here we ride.

VI

What hand and brain went ever paired?
What heart alike conceived and dared?
What act proved all its thought had been?
What will but felt the fleshly screen?
60   We ride and I see her bosom heave.
There's many a crown for who can reach.
Ten lines, a statesman's life in each!
The flag stuck on a heap of bones,
A soldier's doing! what atones?
65 They scratch his name on the Abbey-stones.
    My riding is better, by their leave.

VII

What does it all mean, poet? Well,
Your brains beat into rhythm, you tell
What we felt only; you expressed
70 You hold things beautiful the best,
    And pace them in rhyme so, side by side.

'T is something, nay 't is much: but then,
Have you yourself what's best for men?
Are you—poor, sick, old ere your time—
75 Nearer one whit your own sublime
Than we who never have turned a rhyme?
    Sing, riding's a joy! For me, I ride.

VIII

And you, great sculptor—so, you gave
A score of years to Art, her slave,
80 And that's your Venus, whence we turn
To yonder girl that fords the burn!
    You acquiesce, and shall I repine?
What, man of music, you grown grey
With notes and nothing else to say,
85 Is this your sole praise from a friend,
'Greatly his opera's strains intend,
But in music we know how fashions end!'
    I gave my youth; but we ride, in fine.

IX

Who knows what's fit for us? Had fate
90 Proposed bliss here should sublimate
My being—had I signed the bond—
Still one must lead some life beyond,
    Have a bliss to die with, dim-descried.
This foot once planted on the goal,
95 This glory-garland round my soul,
Could I descry such? Try and test!
I sink back shuddering from the quest.
Earth being so good, would heaven seem best?
    Now, heaven and she are beyond this ride.

X

100 And yet—she has not spoke so long!
What if heaven be that, fair and strong
At life's best, with our eyes upturned
Whither life's flower is first discerned,
    We, fixed so, ever should so abide?
105 What if we still ride on, we two,
With life for ever old yet new,
Changed not in kind but in degree,
The instant made eternity,—
And heaven just prove that I and she
110   Ride, ride together, for ever ride?

The Lost Mistress

I

All's over, then: does truth sound bitter
    As one at first believes?
Hark, 't is the sparrows' good-night twitter
    About your cottage eaves!

II

5 And the leaf-buds on the vine are woolly,
    I noticed that, to-day;
One day more bursts them open fully
    —You know the red turns grey.

III

To-morrow we meet the same then, dearest?
10   May I take your hand in mine?
Mere friends are we,—well, friends the merest
    Keep much that I resign:

IV

For each glance of the eye so bright and black,
    Though I keep with heart's endeavour,—
15 Your voice, when you wish the snowdrops back,
    Though it stay in my soul for ever!—

V

Yet I will but say what mere friends say,
    Or only a thought stronger;
I will hold your hand but as long as all may,
20   Or so very little longer!

The Patriot

An Old Story

I

It was roses, roses, all the way,
    With myrtle mixed in my path like mad:
The house-roofs seemed to heave and sway,
    The church-spires flamed, such flags they had,
5   A year ago on this very day.

II

The air broke into a mist with bells,
    The old walls rocked with the crowd and cries.
Had I said, 'Good folk, mere noise repels –
    But give me your sun from yonder skies!'
10 They had answered, 'And afterward, what else?'

III

Alack, it was I who leaped at the sun
    To give it my loving friends to keep!
Naught man could do, have I left undone:
    And you see my harvest, what I reap
15 This very day, now a year is run.

IV

There's nobody on the house-tops now –
    Just a palsied few at the windows set;
For the best of the sight is, all allow,
    At the Shambles' Gate – or, better yet,
20 By the very scaffold's foot, I trow.

V

I go in the rain, and, more than needs,
    A rope cuts both my wrists behind;
And I think, by the feel, my forehead bleeds,
    For they fling, whoever has a mind,
25 Stones at me for my year's misdeeds.

VI

Thus I entered, and thus I go!
    In triumphs, people have dropped down dead.
'Paid by the world, what dost thou owe
    Me?' – God might question; now instead,
30 'T is God shall repay: I am safer so.

You'll Love Me Yet

You'll love me yet!—and I can tarry
    Your love's protracted growing:
June reared that bunch of flowers you carry,
    From seeds of April's sowing.

5 I plant a heartful now: some seed
    At least is sure to strike,
And yield—what you'll not pluck indeed,
    Not love, but, may be, like.

You'll look at least on love's remains,
10   A grave's one violet:
Your look?—that pays a thousand pains.
    What's death? You'll love me yet!

Geoffrey Chaucer

General Prologue to the Canterbury Tales

Here bygynneth the Book of the Tales of Caunterbury.

    Whan that Aprill with his shoures soote
The droghte of March hath perced to the roote,
And bathed every veyne in swich licour
Of which vertu engendred is the flour;
5 Whan Zephirus eek with his sweete breeth
Inspired hath in every holt and heeth
The tendre croppes, and the yonge sonne
Hath in the Ram his half cours yronne,
And smale foweles maken melodye,
10 That slepen al the nyght with open ye
(So priketh hem nature in hir corages),
Thanne longen folk to goon on pilgrimages,
And palmeres for to seken straunge strondes,
To ferne halwes, kowthe in sondry londes;
15 And specially from every shires ende
Of Engelond to Caunterbury they wende,
The hooly blisful martir for to seke,
That hem hath holpen whan that they were seeke.
    Bifil that in that seson on a day,
20 In Southwerk at the Tabard as I lay
Redy to wenden on my pilgrymage
To Caunterbury with ful devout corage,
At nyght was come into that hostelrye
Wel nyne and twenty in a compaignye
25 Of sondry folk, by aventure yfalle
In felaweshipe, and pilgrimes were they alle,
That toward Caunterbury wolden ryde.
The chambres and the stables weren wyde,
And wel we weren esed atte beste.
30 And shortly, whan the sonne was to reste,
So hadde I spoken with hem everichon
That I was of hir felaweshipe anon,
And made forward erly for to ryse,
To take oure wey ther as I yow devyse.
35   But nathelees, whil I have tyme and space,
Er that I ferther in this tale pace,
Me thynketh it acordaunt to resoun
To telle yow al the condicioun
Of ech of hem, so as it semed me,
40 And whiche they weren, and of what degree,

And eek in what array that they were inne;
And at a knyght than wol I first bigynne.
    A Knyght ther was, and that a worthy man,
That fro the tyme that he first bigan
45 To riden out, he loved chivalrie,
Trouthe and honour, fredom and curteisie.
Ful worthy was he in his lordes werre,
And therto hadde he riden, no man ferre,
As wel in cristendom as in hethenesse,
50 And evere honoured for his worthynesse;
At Alisaundre he was whan it was wonne.
Ful ofte tyme he hadde the bord bigonne
Aboven alle nacions in Pruce;
In Lettow hadde he reysed and in Ruce,
55 No Cristen man so ofte of his degree.
In Gernade at the seege eek hadde he be
Of Algezir, and riden in Belmarye.
At Lyeys was he and at Satalye,
Whan they were wonne, and in the Grete See
60 At many a noble armee hadde he be.
At mortal batailles hadde he been fiftene,
And foughten for oure feith at Tramyssene
In lystes thries, and ay slayn his foo.
This ilke worthy knyght hadde been also
65 Somtyme with the lord of Palatye
Agayn another hethen in Turkye;
And everemoore he hadde a sovereyn prys.
And though that he were worthy, he was wys,
And of his port as meeke as is a mayde.
70 He nevere yet no vileynye ne sayde
In al his lyf unto no maner wight.
He was a verray, parfit gentil knyght.
But for to tellen yow of his array,
His hors were goode, but he was nat gay.
75 Of fustian he wered a gypon
Al bismotered with his habergeon,
For he was late ycome from his viage,
And wente for to doon his pilgrymage.
    With hym ther was his sone, a yong Squier,
80 A lovyere and a lusty bacheler,
With lokkes crulle as they were leyd in presse.
Of twenty yeer of age he was, I gesse.
Of his stature he was of evene lengthe,
And wonderly delyvere, and of greet strengthe.

85 And he hadde been somtyme in chyvachie
In Flaundres, in Artoys, and Pycardie,
And born hym weel, as of so litel space,
In hope to stonden in his lady grace.
Embrouded was he, as it were a meede
90 Al ful of fresshe floures, whyte and reede.
Syngynge he was, or floytynge, al the day;
He was as fressh as is the month of May.
Short was his gowne, with sleves longe and wyde.
Wel koude he sitte on hors and faire ryde.
95 He koude songes make and wel endite,
Juste and eek daunce, and weel purtreye and write.
So hoote he lovede that by nyghtertale
He sleep namoore than dooth a nyghtyngale.
Curteis he was, lowely, and servysable,
100 And carf biforn his fader at the table.

A YEMAN hadde he and servantz namo
At that tyme, for hym liste ride so,
And he was clad in cote and hood of grene.
A sheef of pecok arwes, bright and kene,
105 Under his belt he bar ful thriftily
(Wel koude he dresse his takel yemanly;
His arwes drouped noght with fetheres lowe),
And in his hand he baar a myghty bowe.
A not heed hadde he, with a broun visage.
110 Of wodecraft wel koude he al the usage.
Upon his arm he baar a gay bracer,
And by his syde a swerd and a bokeler,
And on that oother syde a gay daggere
Harneised wel and sharp as point of spere;
115 A Cristopher on his brest of silver sheene.
An horn he bar, the bawdryk was of grene;
A forster was he, soothly, as I gesse.

Ther was also a Nonne, a PRIORESSE,
That of hir smylyng was ful symple and coy;
120 Hire gretteste ooth was but by Seinte Loy;
And she was cleped madame Eglentyne.
Ful weel she soong the service dyvyne,
Entuned in hir nose ful semely;
And Frenssh she spak ful faire and fetisly,
125 After the scole of Stratford atte Bowe,
For Frenssh of Parys was to hire unknowe.
At mete wel ytaught was she with alle;
She leet no morsel from hir lippes falle,

Ne wette hir fyngres in hir sauce depe;
130 Wel koude she carie a morsel and wel kepe
That no drope ne fille upon hire brest.
In curteisie was set ful muchel hir lest.
Hir over-lippe wyped she so clene
That in hir coppe ther was no ferthyng sene
135 Of grece, whan she dronken hadde hir draughte.
Ful semely after hir mete she raughte.
And sikerly she was of greet desport,
And ful plesaunt, and amyable of port,
And peyned hire to countrefete cheere
140 Of court, and to been estatlich of manere,
And to ben holden digne of reverence.
But for to speken of hire conscience,
She was so charitable and so pitous
She wolde wepe, if that she saugh a mous
145 Kaught in a trappe, if it were deed or bledde.
Of smale houndes hadde she that she fedde
With rosted flessh, or milk and wastel-breed.
But soore wepte she if oon of hem were deed,
Or if men smoot it with a yerde smerte;
150 And al was conscience and tendre herte.
Ful semyly hir wympul pynched was,
Hir nose tretys, hir eyen greye as glas,
Hir mouth ful smal, and therto softe and reed.
But sikerly she hadde a fair forheed;
155 It was almoost a spanne brood, I trowe;
For, hardily, she was nat undergrowe.
Ful fetys was hir cloke, as I was war.
Of smal coral aboute hire arm she bar
A peire of bedes, gauded al with grene,
160 And theron heng a brooch of gold ful sheene,
On which ther was first write a crowned A,
And after *Amor vincit omnia.*
    Another NONNE with hire hadde she,
That was hir chapeleyne, and preestes thre.
165   A MONK ther was, a fair for the maistrie,
An outridere, that lovede venerie,
A manly man, to been an abbot able.
Ful many a deyntee hors hadde he in stable,
And whan he rood, men myghte his brydel heere
170 Gynglen in a whistlynge wynd als cleere
And eek as loude as dooth the chapel belle
Ther as this lord was kepere of the celle.

The reule of Seint Maure or of Seint Beneit—
By cause that it was old and somdel streit
175 This ilke Monk leet olde thynges pace,
And heeld after the newe world the space.
He yaf nat of that text a pulled hen,
That seith that hunters ben nat hooly men,
Ne that a monk, whan he is recchelees,
180 Is likned til a fissh that is waterlees—
This is to seyn, a monk out of his cloystre.
But thilke text heeld he nat worth an oystre;
And I seyde his opinion was good.
What sholde he studie and make hymselven wood,
185 Upon a book in cloystre alwey to poure,
Or swynken with his handes, and laboure,
As Austyn bit? How shal the world be served?
Lat Austyn have his swynk to hym reserved!
Therfore he was a prikasour aright:
190 Grehoundes he hadde as swift as fowel in flight;
Of prikyng and of huntyng for the hare
Was al his lust, for no cost wolde he spare.
I seigh his sleves purfiled at the hond
With grys, and that the fyneste of a lond;
195 And for to festne his hood under his chyn,
He hadde of gold ywroght a ful curious pyn;
A love-knotte in the gretter ende ther was.
His heed was balled, that shoon as any glas,
And eek his face, as he hadde been enoynt.
200 He was a lord ful fat and in good poynt;
His eyen stepe, and rollynge in his heed,
That stemed as a forneys of a leed;
His bootes souple, his hors in greet estaat.
Now certeinly he was a fair prelaat;
205 He was nat pale as a forpyned goost.
A fat swan loved he best of any roost.
His palfrey was as broun as is a berye.
        A FRERE ther was, a wantowne and a merye,
A lymytour, a ful solempne man.
210 In alle the ordres foure is noon that kan
So muchel of daliaunce and fair langage.
He hadde maad ful many a mariage
Of yonge wommen at his owene cost.
Unto his ordre he was a noble post.
215 Ful wel biloved and famulier was he
With frankeleyns over al in his contree,
And eek with worthy wommen of the toun;
For he hadde power of confessioun,

As seyde hymself, moore than a curat,
220 For of his ordre he was licenciat.
Ful swetely herde he confessioun,
And plesaunt was his absolucioun:
He was an esy man to yeve penaunce,
Ther as he wiste to have a good pitaunce.
225 For unto a povre ordre for to yive
Is signe that a man is wel yshryve;
For if he yaf, he dorste make avaunt,
He wiste that a man was repentaunt;
For many a man so hard is of his herte,
230 He may nat wepe, althogh hym soore smerte.
Therfore in stede of wepynge and preyeres
Men moote yeve silver to the povre freres.
His typet was ay farsed ful of knyves
And pynnes, for to yeven faire wyves.
235 And certeinly he hadde a murye note:
Wel koude he synge and pleyen on a rote;
Of yeddynges he baar outrely the pris.
His nekke whit was as the flour-de-lys;
Therto he strong was as a champioun.
240 He knew the tavernes wel in every toun
And everich hostiler and tappestere
Bet than a lazar or a beggestere,
For unto swich a worthy man as he
Acorded nat, as by his facultee,
245 To have with sike lazars aqueyntaunce.
It is nat honest; it may nat avaunce,
For to deelen with no swich poraille,
But al with riche and selleres of vitaille.
And over al, ther as profit sholde arise,
250 Curteis he was and lowely of servyse;
Ther nas no man nowher so vertuous.
He was the beste beggere in his hous;
252a [And yaf a certeyn ferme for the graunt;
252b Noon of his bretheren cam ther in his haunt;]
For thogh a wydwe hadde noght a sho,
So plesaunt was his "*In principio*",
255 Yet wolde he have a ferthyng, er he wente.
His purchas was wel bettre than his rente.
And rage he koude, as it were right a whelp.
In love-dayes ther koude he muchel help,
For ther he was nat lyk a cloysterer
260 With a thredbare cope, as is a povre scoler,

But he was lyk a maister or a pope.

Of double worstede was his semycope,

That rounded as a belle out of the presse.

Somwhat he lipsed, for his wantownesse,

265 To make his Englissh sweete upon his tonge;

And in his harpyng, whan that he hadde songe,

His eyen twynkled in his heed aryght

As doon the sterres in the frosty nyght.

This worthy lymytour was cleped Huberd.

270   A MARCHANT was ther with a forked berd,

In mottelee, and hye on horse he sat;

Upon his heed a Flaundryssh bever hat,

His bootes clasped faire and fetisly.

His resons he spak ful solempnely,

275 Sownynge alwey th'encrees of his wynnyng.

He wolde the see were kept for any thyng

Bitwixe Middelburgh and Orewelle.

Wel koude he in eschaunge sheeldes selle.

This worthy man ful wel his wit bisette:

280 Ther wiste no wight that he was in dette,

So estatly was he of his governaunce

With his bargaynes and with his chevyssaunce.

For sothe he was a worthy man with alle,

But, sooth to seyn, I noot how men hym calle.

285   A CLERK ther was of Oxenford also,

That unto logyk hadde longe ygo.

As leene was his hors as is a rake,

And he nas nat right fat, I undertake,

But looked holwe, and therto sobrely.

290 Ful thredbare was his overeste courtepy,

For he hadde geten hym yet no benefice,

Ne was so worldly for to have office.

For hym was levere have at his beddes heed

Twenty bookes, clad in blak or reed,

295 Of Aristotle and his philosophie

Than robes riche, or fithele, or gay sautrie.

But al be that he was a philosophre,

Yet hadde he but litel gold in cofre;

But al that he myghte of his freendes hente,

300 On bookes and on lernynge he it spente,

And bisily gan for the soules preye

Of hem that yaf hym wherwith to scoleye.

Of studie took he moost cure and moost heede,

Noght o word spak he moore than was neede,

305 And that was seyd in forme and reverence,
And short and quyk and ful of hy sentence;
Sownynge in moral vertu was his speche,
And gladly wolde he lerne and gladly teche.
  A SERGEANT OF THE LAWE, war and wys,
310 That often hadde been at the Parvys,
Ther was also, ful riche of excellence.
Discreet he was and of greet reverence—
He semed swich, his wordes weren so wise.
Justice he was ful often in assise,
315 By patente and by pleyn commissioun.
For his science and for his heigh renoun,
Of fees and robes hadde he many oon.
So greet a purchasour was nowher noon:
Al was fee symple to hym in effect;
320 His purchasyng myghte nat been infect.
Nowher so bisy a man as he ther nas,
And yet he semed bisier than he was.
In termes hadde he caas and doomes alle
That from the tyme of kyng William were falle.
325 Therto he koude endite and make a thyng,
Ther koude no wight pynche at his writyng;
And every statut koude he pleyn by rote.
He rood but hoomly in a medlee cote,
Girt with a ceint of silk, with barres smale;
330 Of his array telle I no lenger tale.
  A FRANKELEYN was in his compaignye.
Whit was his berd as is the dayesye;
Of his complexioun he was sangwyn.
Wel loved he by the morwe a sop in wyn;
335 To lyven in delit was evere his wone,
For he was Epicurus owene sone,
That heeld opinioun that pleyn delit
Was verray felicitee parfit.
An housholdere, and that a greet, was he;
340 Seint Julian he was in his contree.
His breed, his ale, was alweys after oon;
A bettre envyned man was nowher noon.
Withoute bake mete was nevere his hous,
Of fissh and flessh, and that so plentevous
345 It snewed in his hous of mete and drynke;
Of alle deyntees that men koude thynke,
After the sondry sesons of the yeer,
So chaunged he his mete and his soper.

Ful many a fat partrich hadde he in muwe,

350 And many a breem and many a luce in stuwe.

Wo was his cook but if his sauce were

Poynaunt and sharp, and redy al his geere.

His table dormant in his halle alway

Stood redy covered al the longe day.

355 At sessiouns ther was he lord and sire;

Ful ofte tyme he was knyght of the shire.

An anlaas and a gipser al of silk

Heeng at his girdel, whit as morne milk.

A shirreve hadde he been, and a contour.

360 Was nowher swich a worthy vavasour.

  An HABERDASSHERE and a CARPENTER,

A WEBBE, a DYERE, and a TAPYCER—

And they were clothed alle in o lyveree

Of a solempne and a greet fraternitee.

365 Ful fressh and newe hir geere apiked was;

Hir knyves were chaped noght with bras

But al with silver, wroght ful clene and weel,

Hire girdles and hir pouches everydeel.

Wel semed ech of hem a fair burgeys

370 To sitten in a yeldehalle on a deys.

Everich, for the wisdom that he kan,

Was shaply for to been an alderman.

For catel hadde they ynogh and rente,

And eek hir wyves wolde it wel assente;

375 And elles certeyn were they to blame.

It is ful fair to been ycleped "madame,"

And goon to vigilies al bifore,

And have a mantel roialliche ybore.

  A COOK they hadde with hem for the nones

380 To boille the chiknes with the marybones,

And poudre-marchant tart and galyngale.

Wel koude he knowe a draughte of Londoun ale.

He koude rooste, and sethe, and broille, and frye,

Maken mortreux, and wel bake a pye.

385 But greet harm was it, as it thoughte me,

That on his shyne a mormal hadde he.

For blankmanger, that made he with the beste.

  A SHIPMAN was ther, wonynge fer by weste;

For aught I woot, he was of Dertemouthe.

390 He rood upon a rouncy, as he kouthe,

In a gowne of faldyng to the knee.

A daggere hangynge on a laas hadde he

Aboute his nekke, under his arm adoun.
The hoote somer hadde maad his hewe al broun;
395 And certeinly he was a good felawe.
Ful many a draughte of wyn had he ydrawe
Fro Burdeux-ward, whil that the chapman sleep.
Of nyce conscience took he no keep.
If that he faught and hadde the hyer hond,
400 By water he sente hem hoom to every lond.
But of his craft to rekene wel his tydes,
His stremes, and his daungers hym bisides,
His herberwe, and his moone, his lodemenage,
Ther nas noon swich from Hulle to Cartage.
405 Hardy he was and wys to undertake;
With many a tempest hadde his berd been shake.
He knew alle the havenes, as they were,
Fro Gootlond to the cape of Fynystere,
And every cryke in Britaigne and in Spayne.
410 His barge ycleped was the Maudelayne.

 With us ther was a DOCTOUR OF PHISIK;
In al this world ne was ther noon hym lik,
To speke of phisik and of surgerye,
For he was grounded in astronomye.
415 He kepte his pacient a ful greet deel
In houres by his magyk natureel.
Wel koude he fortunen the ascendent
Of his ymages for his pacient.
He knew the cause of everich maladye,
420 Were it of hoot, or coold, or moyste, or drye,
And where they engendred, and of what humour.
He was a verray, parfit praktisour:
The cause yknowe, and of his harm the roote,
Anon he yaf the sike man his boote.
425 Ful redy hadde he his apothecaries
To sende hym drogges and his letuaries,
For ech of hem made oother for to wynne—
Hir frendshipe nas nat newe to bigynne.
Wel knew he the olde Esculapius,
430 And Deyscorides, and eek Rufus,
Olde Ypocras, Haly, and Galyen,
Serapion, Razis, and Avycen,
Averrois, Damascien, and Constantyn,
Bernard, and Gatesden, and Gilbertyn.
435 Of his diete mesurable was he,
For it was of no superfluitee,

But of greet norissyng and digestible.

His studie was but litel on the Bible.

In sangwyn and in pers he clad was al,

440 Lyned with taffata and with sendal.

And yet he was but esy of dispence;

He kepte that he wan in pestilence.

For gold in phisik is a cordial,

Therefore he lovede gold in special.

445   A good WIF was ther OF biside BATHE,

But she was somdel deef, and that was scathe.

Of clooth-makyng she hadde swich an haunt

She passed hem of Ypres and of Gaunt.

In al the parisshe wif ne was ther noon

450 That to the offrynge bifore hire sholde goon;

And if ther dide, certeyn so wrooth was she

That she was out of alle charitee.

Hir coverchiefs ful fyne weren of ground;

I dorste swere they weyeden ten pound

455 That on a Sonday weren upon hir heed.

Hir hosen weren of fyn scarlet reed,

Ful streite yteyd, and shoes ful moyste and newe.

Boold was hir face, and fair, and reed of hewe.

She was a worthy womman al hir lyve:

460 Housbondes at chirche dore she hadde fyve,

Withouten oother compaignye in youthe—

But thereof nedeth nat to speke as nowthe.

And thries hadde she been at Jerusalem;

She hadde passed many a straunge strem;

465 At Rome she hadde been, and at Boloigne,

In Galice at Seint-Jame, and at Coloigne.

She koude muchel of wandrynge by the weye.

Gat-tothed was she, soothly for to seye.

Upon an amblere esily she sat,

470 Ywympled wel, and on hir heed an hat

As brood as is a bokeler or a targe;

A foot-mantel aboute hir hipes large,

And on hir feet a paire of spores sharpe.

In felaweshipe wel koude she laughe and carpe.

475 Of remedies of love she knew per chaunce,

For she koude of that art the olde daunce.

    A good man was ther of religioun,

And was a povre PERSOUN OF A TOUN,

But riche he was of hooly thoght and werk.

480 He was also a lerned man, a clerk,

That Cristes gospel trewely wolde preche;
His parisshens devoutly wolde he teche.
Benygne he was, and wonder diligent,
And in adversitee ful pacient,
485 And swich he was ypreved ofte sithes.
Ful looth were hym to cursen for his tithes,
But rather wolde he yeven, out of doute,
Unto his povre parisshens aboute
Of his offryng and eek of his substaunce.
490 He koude in litel thyng have suffisaunce.
Wyd was his parisshe, and houses fer asonder,
But he ne lefte nat, for reyn ne thonder,
In siknesse nor in meschief to visite
The ferreste in his parisshe, muche and lite,
495 Upon his feet, and in his hand a staf.
This noble ensample to his sheep he yaf,
That first he wroghte, and afterward he taughte.
Out of the gospel he tho wordes caughte,
And this figure he added eek therto,
500 That if gold ruste, what shal iren do?
For if a preest be foul, on whom we truste,
No wonder is a lewed man to ruste;
And shame it is, if a prest take keep,
A shiten shepherde and a clene sheep.
505 Wel oghte a preest ensample for to yive,
By his clennesse, how that his sheep sholde lyve.
He sette nat his benefice to hyre
And leet his sheep encombred in the myre
And ran to Londoun unto Seinte Poules
510 To seken hym a chaunterie for soules,
Or with a bretherhed to been withholde;
But dwelte at hoom, and kepte wel his folde,
So that the wolf ne made it nat myscarie;
He was a shepherde and noght a mercenarie.
515 And though he hooly were and vertuous,
He was to synful men nat despitous,
Ne of his speche daungerous ne digne,
But in his techyng discreet and benygne.
To drawen folk to hevene by fairnesse,
520 By good ensample, this was his bisynesse.
But it were any persone obstinat,
What so he were, of heigh or lough estat,
Hym wolde he snybben sharply for the nonys.
A bettre preest I trowe that nowher noon ys.

525 He waited after no pompe and reverence,
Ne maked him a spiced conscience,
But Cristes loore and his apostles twelve
He taughte; but first he folwed it hymselve.
    With hym ther was a PLOWMAN, was his brother,
530 That hadde ylad of dong ful many a fother;
A trewe swynkere and a good was he,
Lyvynge in pees and parfit charitee.
God loved he best with al his hoole herte
At alle tymes, thogh him gamed or smerte,
535 And thanne his neighebor right as hymselve.
He wolde thresshe, and therto dyke and delve,
For Cristes sake, for every povre wight,
Withouten hire, if it lay in his myght. .
His tithes payde he ful faire and wel,
540 Bothe of his propre swynk and his catel.
In a tabard he rood upon a mere.
    Ther was also a REVE, and a MILLERE,
A SOMNOUR, and a PARDONER also,
A MAUNCIPLE, and myself—ther were namo.
545   The MILLERE was a stout carl for the nones;
Ful byg he was of brawn, and eek of bones.
That proved wel, for over al ther he cam,
At wrastlynge he wolde have alwey the ram.
He was short-sholdred, brood, a thikke knarre;
550 Ther was no dore that he nolde heve of harre,
Or breke it at a rennyng with his heed.
His berd as any sowe or fox was reed,
And therto brood, as though it were a spade.
Upon the cop right of his nose he hade
555 A werte, and theron stood a toft of herys,
Reed as the brustles of a sowes erys;
His nosethirles blake were and wyde.
A swerd and a bokeler bar he by his syde.
His mouth as greet was as a greet forneys.
560 He was a janglere and a goliardeys,
And that was moost of synne and harlotries.
Wel koude he stelen corn and tollen thries;
And yet he hadde a thombe of gold, pardee.
A whit cote and a blew hood wered he.
565 A baggepipe wel koude he blowe and sowne,
And therwithal he broghte us out of towne.
    A gentil MAUNCIPLE was ther of a temple,
Of which achatours myghte take exemple
For to be wise in byynge of vitaille;
570 For wheither that he payde or took by taille,

Algate he wayted so in his achaat
That he was ay biforn and in good staat.
Now is nat that of God a ful fair grace
That swich a lewed mannes wit shal pace
575 The wisdom of an heep of lerned men?
Of maistres hadde he mo than thries ten,
That weren of lawe expert and curious,
Of which ther were a duszeyne in that hous
Worthy to been stywardes of rente and lond
580 Of any lord that is in Engelond,
To make hym lyve by his propre good
In honour dettelees (but if he were wood),
Or lyve as scarsly as hym list desire;
And able for to helpen al a shire
585 In any caas that myghte falle or happe.
And yet this Manciple sette hir aller cappe.
      The Reve was a sclendre colerik man.
His berd was shave as ny as ever he kan;
His heer was by his erys ful round yshorn;
590 His top was dokked lyk a preest biforn.
Ful longe were his legges and ful lene,
Ylyk a staf; ther was no calf ysene.
Wel koude he kepe a gerner and a bynne;
Ther was noon auditour koude on him wynne.
595 Wel wiste he by the droghte and by the reyn
The yeldynge of his seed and of his greyn.
His lordes sheep, his neet, his dayerye,
His swyn, his hors, his stoor, and his pultrye
Was hoolly in this Reves governynge,
600 And by his covenant yaf the rekenynge,
Syn that his lord was twenty yeer of age.
Ther koude no man brynge hym in arrerage.
Ther nas baillif, ne hierde, nor oother hyne,
That he ne knew his sleighte and his covyne;
605 They were adrad of hym as of the deeth.
His wonyng was ful faire upon an heeth;
With grene trees yshadwed was his place.
He koude bettre than his lord purchace.
Ful riche he was astored pryvely.
610 His lord wel koude he plesen subtilly,
To yeve and lene hym of his owene good,
And have a thank, and yet a cote and hood.
In youthe he hadde lerned a good myster:
He was a wel good wrighte, a carpenter.

615 This Reve sat upon a ful good stot

That was al pomely grey and highte Scot.

A long surcote of pers upon he hade,

And by his syde he baar a rusty blade.

Of Northfolk was this Reve of which I telle,

620 Biside a toun men clepen Baldeswelle.

Tukked he was as is a frere aboute,

And evere he rood the hyndreste of oure route.

    A Somonour was ther with us in that place,

That hadde a fyr-reed cherubynnes face,

625 For saucefleem he was, with eyen narwe.

As hoot he was and lecherous as a sparwe,

With scalled browes blake and piled berd.

Of his visage children were aferd.

Ther nas quyk-silver, lytarge, ne brymstoon,

630 Boras, ceruce, ne oille of tartre noon,

Ne oynement that wolde clense and byte,

That hym myghte helpen of his whelkes white,

Nor of the knobbes sittynge on his chekes.

Wel loved he garleek, oynons, and eek lekes,

635 And for to drynken strong wyn, reed as blood;

Thanne wolde he speke and crie as he were wood.

And whan that he wel dronken hadde the wyn,

Thanne wolde he speke no word but Latyn.

A fewe termes hadde he, two or thre,

640 That he had lerned out of som decree—

No wonder is, he herde it al the day;

And eek ye knowen wel how that a jay

Kan clepen "Watte" as wel as kan the pope.

But whoso koude in oother thyng hym grope,

645 Thanne hadde he spent al his philosophie;

Ay "*Questio quid iuris*" wolde he crie.

He was a gentil harlot and a kynde;

A bettre felawe sholde men noght fynde.

He wolde suffre for a quart of wyn

650 A good felawe to have his concubyn

A twelf month, and excuse hym atte fulle;

Ful prively a fynch eek koude he pulle.

And if he foond owher a good felawe,

He wolde techen him to have noon awe

655 In swich caas of the ercedekenes curs,

But if a mannes soule were in his purs;

For in his purs he sholde ypunysshed be.

"Purs is the ercedekenes helle," seyde he.

But wel I woot he lyed right in dede;

660 Of cursyng oghte ech gilty man him drede,

For curs wol slee right as assoillyng savith,
And also war hym of a *Significavit*.
In daunger hadde he at his owene gise
The yonge girles of the diocise,
665 And knew hir conseil, and was al hir reed.
A gerland hadde he set upon his heed,
As greet as it were for an ale-stake.
A bokeleer hadde he maad hym of a cake.
    With hym ther rood a gentil PARDONER
670 Of Rouncivale, his freend and his compeer,
That streight was comen fro the court of Rome.
Ful loude he soong "Com hider, love, to me!"
This Somonour bar to hym a stif burdoun;
Was nevere trompe of half so greet a soun.
675 This Pardoner hadde heer as yelow as wex,
But smothe it heeng as dooth a strike of flex;
By ounces henge his lokkes that he hadde,
And therwith he his shuldres overspradde;
But thynne it lay, by colpons oon and oon.
680 But hood, for jolitee, wered he noon,
For it was trussed up in his walet.
Hym thoughte he rood al of the newe jet;
Dischevelee, save his cappe, he rood al bare.
Swiche glarynge eyen hadde he as an hare.
685 A vernycle hadde he sowed upon his cappe.
His walet, biforn hym in his lappe,
Bretful of pardoun comen from Rome al hoot.
A voys he hadde as smal as hath a goot.
No berd hadde he, ne nevere sholde have;
690 As smothe it was as it were late shave.
I trowe he were a geldyng or a mare.
But of his craft, fro Berwyk into Ware
Ne was ther swich another pardoner.
For in his male he hadde a pilwe-beer,
695 Which that he seyde was Oure Lady veyl;
He seyde he hadde a gobet of the seyl
That Seint Peter hadde, whan that he wente
Upon the see, til Jhesu Crist hym hente.
He hadde a croys of latoun ful of stones,
700 And in a glas he hadde pigges bones.
But with thise relikes, whan that he fond
A povre person dwellynge upon lond,
Upon a day he gat hym moore moneye
Than that the person gat in monthes tweye;

705 And thus, with feyned flaterye and japes,
　　He made the person and the peple his apes.
　　But trewely to tellen atte laste,
　　He was in chirche a noble ecclesiaste.
　　Wel koude he rede a lessoun or a storie,
710 But alderbest he song an offertorie;
　　For wel he wiste, whan that song was songe,
　　He moste preche and wel affile his tonge
　　To wynne silver, as he ful wel koude;
　　Therefore he song the murierly and loude.
715 　　Now have I toold you soothly, in a clause,
　　Th'estaat, th'array, the nombre, and eek the cause
　　Why that assembled was this compaignye
　　In Southwerk at this gentil hostelrye
　　That highte the Tabard, faste by the Belle.
720 But now is tyme to yow for to telle
　　How that we baren us that ilke nyght,
　　Whan we were in that hostelrie alyght;
　　And after wol I telle of our viage
　　And al the remenaunt of oure pilgrimage.
725 But first I pray yow, of youre curteisye,
　　That ye n'arette it nat my vileynye,
　　Thogh that I pleynly speke in this mateere,
　　To telle yow hir wordes and hir cheere,
　　Ne thogh I speke hir wordes proprely.
730 For this ye knowen al so wel as I:
　　Whoso shal telle a tale after a man,
　　He moot reherce as ny as evere he kan
　　Everich a word, if it be in his charge,
　　Al speke he never so rudeliche and large,
735 Or ellis he moot telle his tale untrewe,
　　Or feyne thyng, or fynde wordes newe.
　　He may nat spare, althogh he were his brother;
　　He moot as wel seye o word as another.
　　Crist spak hymself ful brode in hooly writ,
740 And wel ye woot no vileynye is it.
　　Eek Plato seith, whoso kan hym rede,
　　The wordes moote be cosyn to the dede.
　　Also I prey yow to foryeve it me,
　　Al have I nat set folk in hir degree
745 Heere in this tale, as that they sholde stonde.
　　My wit is short, ye may wel understonde.
　　　　Greet chiere made oure Hoost us everichon,
　　And to the soper sette he us anon.
　　He served us with vitaille at the beste;
750 Strong was the wyn, and wel to drynke us leste.

A semely man OURE HOOSTE was withalle
For to been a marchal in an halle.
A large man he was with eyen stepe—
A fairer burgeys was ther noon in Chepe—
755 Boold of his speche, and wys, and wel ytaught,
And of manhod hym lakkede right naught.
Eek therto he was right a myrie man;
And after soper pleyen he bigan,
And spak of myrthe amonges othere thynges,
760 Whan that we hadde maad oure rekenynges,
And seyde thus: "Now, lordynges, trewely,
Ye been to me right welcome, hertely;
For by my trouthe, if that I shal nat lye,
I saugh nat this yeer so myrie a compaignye
765 Atones in this herberwe as is now.
Fayn wolde I doon yow myrthe, wiste I how.
And of a myrthe I am right now bythoght,
To doon yow ese, and it shal coste noght.
"Ye goon to Caunterbury—God yow speede,
770 The blisful martir quite yow youre meede!
And wel I woot, as ye goon by the weye,
Ye shapen yow to talen and to pleye;
For trewely, confort ne myrthe is noon
To ride by the weye doumb as a stoon;
775 And therfore wol I maken yow disport,
As I seyde erst, and doon yow som confort.
And if yow liketh alle by oon assent
For to stonden at my juggement,
And for to werken as I shal yow seye,
780 Tomorwe, whan ye riden by the weye,
Now, by my fader soule that is deed,
But ye be myrie, I wol yeve yow myn heed!
Hoold up youre hondes, withouten moore speche."
Oure conseil was nat longe for to seche.
785 Us thoughte it was noght worth to make it wys,
And graunted hym withouten moore avys,
And bad him seye his voirdit as hym leste.
"Lordynges," quod he, "now herkneth for the beste;
But taak it nought, I prey yow, in desdeyn.
790 This is the poynt, to speken short and pleyn,
That ech of yow, to shorte with oure weye,
In this viage shal telle tales tweye
To Caunterbury-ward, I mene it so,
And homward he shal tellen othere two,

795 Of aventures that whilom han bifalle.
And which of yow that bereth hym best of alle—
That is to seyn, that telleth in this caas
Tales of best sentence and moost solaas—
Shal have a soper at oure aller cost

800 Heere in this place, sittynge by this post,
Whan that we come agayn fro Caunterbury.
And for to make yow the moore mury,
I wol myselven goodly with yow ryde,
Right at myn owene cost, and be youre gyde;

805 And whoso wole my juggement withseye
Shal paye al that we spenden by the weye.
And if ye vouche sauf that it be so,
Tel me anon, withouten wordes mo,
And I wol erly shape me therfore."

810   This thyng was graunted, and oure othes swore
With ful glad herte, and preyden hym also
That he wolde vouche sauf for to do so,
And that he wolde been oure governour,
And of oure tales juge and reportour,

815 And sette a soper at a certeyn pris,
And we wol reuled been at his devys
In heigh and lough; and thus by oon assent
We been acorded to his juggement.
And therupon the wyn was fet anon;

820 We dronken, and to reste wente echon,
Withouten any lenger taryynge.
   Amorwe, whan that day bigan to sprynge,
Up roos oure Hoost, and was oure aller cok,
And gadrede us togidre alle in a flok,

825 And forth we riden a litel moore than paas
Unto the Wateryng of Seint Thomas;
And there oure Hoost bigan his hors areste
And seyde, "Lordynges, herkneth, if yow leste.
Ye woot youre foreward, and I it yow recorde.

830 If even-song and morwe-song accorde,
Lat se now who shal telle the firste tale.
As evere mote I drynke wyn or ale,
Whoso be rebel to my juggement
Shal paye for al that by the wey is spent.

835 Now draweth cut, er that we ferrer twynne;
He which that hath the shorteste shal bigynne.
Sire Knyght," quod he, "my mayster and my lord,
Now draweth cut, for that is myn accord.

Cometh neer," quod he, "my lady Prioresse.
840 And ye, sire Clerk, lat be youre shamefastnesse,
Ne studieth noght; ley hond to, every man!"
Anon to drawen every wight bigan,
And shortly for to tellen as it was,
Were it by aventure, or sort, or cas,
845 The sothe is this: the cut fil to the Knyght,
Of which ful blithe and glad was every wyght,
And telle he moste his tale, as was resoun,
By foreward and by composicioun,
As ye han herd; what nedeth wordes mo?
850 And whan this goode man saugh that it was so,
As he that wys was and obedient
To kepe his foreward by his free assent,
He seyde, "Syn I shal bigynne the game,
What, welcome be the cut, a Goddes name!
855 Now lat us ryde, and herkneth what I seye."
And with that word we ryden forth oure weye,
And he bigan with right a myrie cheere
His tale anon, and seyde as ye may heere.

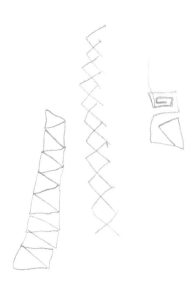

Thomas Hardy

A Broken Appointment

You did not come,
And marching Time drew on, and wore me numb. —
Yet less for loss of your dear presence there
Than that I thus found lacking in your make
5 That high compassion which can overbear
Reluctance for pure lovingkindness' sake
Grieved I, when, as the hope-hour stroked its sum,
You did not come.

You love not me,
10 And love alone can lend you loyalty;
– I know and knew it. But, unto the store
Of human deeds divine in all but name,
Was it not worth a little hour or more
To add yet this: Once you, a woman, came
15 To soothe a time-torn man; even though it be
You love not me?

Drummer Hodge

I

They throw in Drummer Hodge, to rest
Uncoffined – just as found:
His landmark is a kopje-crest
That breaks the veldt around;
5 And foreign constellations west
Each night above his mound.

II

Young Hodge the Drummer never knew –
Fresh from his Wessex home –
The meaning of the broad Karoo,
10 The Bush, the dusty loam,
And why uprose to nightly view
Strange stars amid the gloom.

III

Yet portion of that unknown plain
Will Hodge for ever be;
15 His homely Northern breast and brain
Grow to some Southern tree,
And strange-eyed constellations reign
His stars eternally.

At Castle Boterel

As I drive to the junction of lane and highway,
    And the drizzle bedrenches the waggonette,
I look behind at the fading byway,
    And see on its slope, now glistening wet,
5   Distinctly yet

Myself and a girlish form benighted
    In dry March weather. We climb the road
Beside a chaise. We had just alighted
    To ease the sturdy pony's load
10   When he sighed and slowed.

What we did as we climbed, and what we talked of
    Matters not much, nor to what it led, –
Something that life will not be balked of
    Without rude reason till hope is dead,
15   And feeling fled.

It filled but a minute. But was there ever
    A time of such quality, since or before,
In that hill's story? To one mind never,
    Though it has been climbed, foot-swift, foot-sore,
20   By thousands more.

Primaeval rocks form the road's steep border,
    And much have they faced there, first and last,
Of the transitory in Earth's long order;
    But what they record in colour and cast
25   Is – that we two passed.

And to me, though Time's unflinching rigour,
    In mindless rote, has ruled from sight
The substance now, one phantom figure
    Remains on the slope, as when that night
30   Saw us alight.

I look and see it there, shrinking, shrinking,
    I look back at it amid the rain
For the very last time; for my sand is sinking.
    And I shall traverse old love's domain
35   Never again.

March 1913

Beeny Cliff

March 1870—March 1913

I

O the opal and the sapphire of that wandering western sea,
And the woman riding high above with bright hair flapping free –
The woman whom I loved so, and who loyally loved me.

II

The pale mews plained below us, and the waves seemed far away
5 In a nether sky, engrossed in saying their ceaseless babbling say,
As we laughed light-heartedly aloft on that clear-sunned March day.

III

A little cloud then cloaked us, and there flew an irised rain,
And the Atlantic dyed its levels with a dull misfeatured stain,
And then the sun burst out again, and purples prinked the main.

IV

10 – Still in all its chasmal beauty bulks old Beeny to the sky,
And shall she and I not go there once again now March is nigh,
And the sweet things said in that March say anew there by and by?

V

What if still in chasmal beauty looms that wild weird western shore,
The woman now is – elsewhere – whom the ambling pony bore,
15 And nor knows nor cares for Beeny, and will laugh there nevermore.

Beyond the Last Lamp

(Near Tooting Common)

I

While rain, with eve in partnership,
Descended darkly, drip, drip, drip,
Beyond the last lone lamp I passed
  Walking slowly, whispering sadly,
5 Two linked loiterers, wan, downcast:
Some heavy thought constrained each face,
And blinded them to time and place.

II

The pair seemed lovers, yet absorbed
In mental scenes no longer orbed
10 By love's young rays. Each countenance
  As it slowly, as it sadly
  Caught the lamplight's yellow glance,
Held in suspense a misery
At things which had been or might be.

III

15 When I retrod that watery way
Some hours beyond the droop of day,
Still I found pacing there the twain
  Just as slowly, just as sadly,
  Heedless of the night and rain.
20 One could but wonder who they were
And what wild woe detained them there.

IV

Though thirty years of blur and blot
Have slid since I beheld that spot,
And saw in curious converse there
25 Moving slowly, moving sadly
  That mysterious tragic pair,
Its olden look may linger on –
All but the couple; they have gone.

V

Whither? Who knows, indeed. . . . And yet
30 To me, when nights are weird and wet,
Without those comrades there at tryst
  Creeping slowly, creeping sadly,
  That lone lane does not exist.
There they seem brooding on their pain,
35 And will, while such a lane remain.

During Wind and Rain

They sing their dearest songs –
He, she, all of them – yea,
Treble and tenor and bass,
   And one to play;
5   With the candles mooning each face. . . .
   Ah, no; the years O!
How the sick leaves reel down in throngs!

They clear the creeping moss –
Elders and juniors – aye,
10   Making the pathways neat
   And the garden gay;
And they build a shady seat. . . .
   Ah, no; the years, the years;
See, the white storm-birds wing across!

15   They are blithely breakfasting all –
Men and maidens – yea,
Under the summer tree,
   With a glimpse of the bay,
While pet fowl come to the knee. . . .
20   Ah, no; the years O!
And the rotten rose is ript from the wall.

They change to a high new house,
He, she, all of them – aye,
Clocks and carpets and chairs
25   On the lawn all day,
And brightest things that are theirs. . . .
   Ah, no; the years, the years;
Down their carved names the rain-drop ploughs.

In Time of 'The Breaking of Nations'

I

Only a man harrowing clods
   In a slow silent walk
With an old horse that stumbles and nods
   Half asleep as they stalk.

II

5 Only thin smoke without flame
   From the heaps of couch-grass;
Yet this will go onward the same
   Though Dynasties pass.

III

Yonder a maid and her wight
10   Come whispering by:
War's annals will cloud into night
   Ere their story die.

1915

[handwritten annotation: contemplation / consider purpose of war after killing / soldier has killed + is contemplating on actions]

The Man He Killed

   'Had he and I but met
   By some old ancient inn,
We should have sat us down to wet
   Right many a nipperkin!

5   'But ranged as infantry,
   And staring face to face,
I shot at him as he at me,
   And killed him in his place.

   'I shot him dead because –
10   Because he was my foe,
Just so: my foe of course he was;
   That's clear enough; although

   'He thought he'd 'list, perhaps,
   Off-hand like – just as I –
15 Was out of work – had sold his traps –
   No other reason why.

   'Yes; quaint and curious war is!
   You shoot a fellow down
You'd treat if met where any bar is,
20   Or help to half-a-crown.'

1902

The Convergence of the Twain

(Lines on the loss of the 'Titanic')

I

In a solitude of the sea
Deep from human vanity,
And the Pride of Life that planned her, stilly couches she.

II

Steel chambers, late the pyres
Of her salamandrine fires,
Cold currents thrid, and turn to rhythmic tidal lyres.

III

Over the mirrors meant
To glass the opulent
The sea-worm crawls – grotesque, slimed, dumb, indifferent.

IV

Jewels in joy designed
To ravish the sensuous mind
Lie lightless, all their sparkles bleared and black and blind.

V

Dim moon-faced fishes near
Gaze at the gilded gear
And query: 'What does this vaingloriousness down here?' . . .

VI

Well: while was fashioning
This creature of cleaving wing,
The Immanent Will that stirs and urges everything

VII

Prepared a sinister mate
For her – so gaily great –
A Shape of Ice, for the time far and dissociate.

VIII

And as the smart ship grew
In stature, grace, and hue,
In shadowy silent distance grew the Iceberg too.

IX

25   Alien they seemed to be:
No mortal eye could see
The intimate welding of their later history,

X

Or sign that they were bent
By paths coincident
30 On being anon twin halves of one august event,

XI

Till the Spinner of the Years
Said 'Now!' And each one hears,
And consummation comes, and jars two hemispheres.

The Darkling Thrush

I leant upon a coppice gate
    When Frost was spectre-gray,
And Winter's dregs made desolate
    The weakening eye of day.
5 The tangled bine-stems scored the sky
    Like strings of broken lyres,
And all mankind that haunted nigh
    Had sought their household fires.

The land's sharp features seemed to be
10   The Century's corpse outleant,
His crypt the cloudy canopy,
    The wind his death-lament.
The ancient pulse of germ and birth
    Was shrunken hard and dry,
15 And every spirit upon earth
    Seemed fervourless as I.

At once a voice arose among
    The bleak twigs overhead
In a full-hearted evensong
20   Of joy illimited;
An aged thrush, frail, gaunt, and small,
    In blast-beruffled plume,
Had chosen thus to fling his soul
    Upon the growing gloom.

25 So little cause for carolings
    Of such ecstatic sound
Was written on terrestrial things
    Afar or nigh around,
That I could think there trembled through
30   His happy good-night air
Some blessed Hope, whereof he knew
    And I was unaware.

31 December 1900

The Going

Why did you give no hint that night
That quickly after the morrow's dawn,
And calmly, as if indifferent quite,
You would close your term here, up and be gone
5   Where I could not follow
      With wing of swallow
To gain one glimpse of you ever anon!

      Never to bid good-bye,
      Or lip me the softest call,
10 Or utter a wish for a word, while I
Saw morning harden upon the wall,
      Unmoved, unknowing
      That your great going
Had place that moment, and altered all.

15 Why do you make me leave the house
And think for a breath it is you I see
At the end of the alley of bending boughs
Where so often at dusk you used to be;
      Till in darkening dankness
20   The yawning blankness
Of the perspective sickens me!

      You were she who abode
      By those red-veined rocks far West,
You were the swan-necked one who rode
25 Along the beetling Beeny Crest,
      And, reining nigh me,
      Would muse and eye me,
While Life unrolled us its very best.

Why, then, latterly did we not speak,
30 Did we not think of those days long dead,
And ere your vanishing strive to seek
That time's renewal? We might have said,
      'In this bright spring weather
      We'll visit together
35 Those places that once we visited.'

      Well, well! All's past amend,
      Unchangeable. It must go.
I seem but a dead man held on end
To sink down soon. . . . O you could not know
40   That such swift fleeing
      No soul foreseeing –
Not even I – would undo me so!

December 1912

The Oxen

Christmas Eve, and twelve of the clock.
   'Now they are all on their knees,'
An elder said as we sat in a flock
   By the embers in hearthside ease.

5 We pictured the meek mild creatures where
   They dwelt in their strawy pen,
Nor did it occur to one of us there
   To doubt they were kneeling then.

So fair a fancy few would weave
10   In these years! Yet, I feel,
If someone said on Christmas Eve,
   'Come; see the oxen kneel

'In the lonely barton by yonder coomb
   Our childhood used to know,'
15 I should go with him in the gloom,
   Hoping it might be so.

1915

Conversati...

BOTH POEMS - 2 SIDES OF HARDY DIRECT SPEECH

The Ruined Maid

lively countrymaid
shameless about what she's done
likeable
jaunty, cheerful playfulness, funny, saucy
unlike rest
shocked at new thing, turned out for her
Rich BF. friend has worked

'O 'Melia, my dear, this does everything crown! *this tops ev. done before*
Who could have supposed I should meet you in Town? *(London)*
And whence such fair garments, such prosperi-ty?' – *where did u get*
'O didn't you know I'd been ruined?' said she. *always has last word - cheeky mischievous*

5 – 'You left us in tatters, without shoes or socks, *cheeky, look what happened to me* *morally, socially - has been a mistress* *doomed*
Tired of digging potatoes, and spudding up docks; *spudding/digging weed - rural expression*
And now you've gay bracelets and bright feathers three!' –
'Yes: that's how we dress when we're ruined,' said she. *Off hand* *red* *to be above her pal* *used to speak as an ignorant rustic*
I belong to diff class *farm (dairy)*

– 'At home in the barton you said "thee" and "thou",
10 And "thik oon", and "theäs oon", and "t'other"; but now
Your talking quite fits 'ee for high compa-ny!' –
'Some polish is gained with one's ruin,' said she. *has met with well off man* *make best out of what she*

– 'Your hands were like paws then, your face blue and bleak
But now I'm bewitched by your delicate cheek, *ironic that she* *but isn't*
15 And your little gloves fit as on any la-dy!' –
'We never do work when we're ruined,' said she.

– 'You used to call home-life a hag-ridden dream,
And you'd sigh, and you'd sock; but at present you seem *to mean - dialect*
To know not of megrims or melancho-ly!' – *local dialect - migraine headache* *miserable state*
20 'True. One's pretty lively when ruined,' said she.

– 'I wish I had feathers, a fine sweeping gown, *ironic she's one too*
And a delicate face, and could strut about Town!' –
'My dear – a raw country girl, such as you be, *condescending not glad to see pal*
Cannot quite expect that. You ain't ruined,' said she.

Westbourne Park Villas, 1866

if you work hard, instead you can... mean = better life

still says West Country expressions - tells us she's not really a lady shows old side deep down she's not.

L: tone of 2 poems - rhythm rhyme etc. = v diff
worth the risk

The Voice

Woman much missed, how you call to me, call to me,
Saying that now you are not as you were
When you had changed from the one who was all to me,
But as at first, when our day was fair.

5 Can it be you that I hear? Let me view you, then,
Standing as when I drew near to the town
Where you would wait for me: yes, as I knew you then,
Even to the original air-blue gown!

Or is it only the breeze, in its listlessness
10 Travelling across the wet mead to me here,
You being ever dissolved to wan wistlessness,
Heard no more again far or near?

    Thus I; faltering forward,
    Leaves around me falling,
15 Wind oozing thin through the thorn from norward,
    And the woman calling.

December 1912

Transformations

    Portion of this yew
    Is a man my grandsire knew,
    Bosomed here at its foot:
    This branch may be his wife,
5 A ruddy human life
    Now turned to a green shoot.

    These grasses must be made
    Of her who often prayed,
    Last century, for repose;
10 And the fair girl long ago
    Whom I often tried to know
    May be entering this rose.

    So, they are not underground,
    But as nerves and veins abound
15 In the growths of upper air,
    And they feel the sun and rain,
    And the energy again
    That made them what they were!

Wilfred Owen

Anthem for Doomed Youth

What passing-bells for these who die as cattle?
   – Only the monstrous anger of the guns.
   Only the stuttering rifles' rapid rattle
Can patter out their hasty orisons.
5 No mockeries now for them; no prayers nor bells;
   Nor any voice of mourning save the choirs, –
The shrill, demented choirs of wailing shells;
   And bugles calling for them from sad shires.

What candles may be held to speed them all?
10   Not in the hands of boys but in their eyes
Shall shine the holy glimmers of goodbyes.
   The pallor of girls' brows shall be their pall;
Their flowers the tenderness of patient minds,
And each slow dusk a drawing-down of blinds.

Conscious

His fingers wake, and flutter; up the bed.
His eyes come open with a pull of will,
Helped by the yellow mayflowers by his head.
The blind-cord drawls across the window-sill . . .
5 What a smooth floor the ward has! What a rug!
Who is that talking somewhere out of sight?
Three flies are creeping round the shiny jug . . .
'Nurse! Doctor!' – 'Yes, all right, all right.'

But sudden evening blurs and fogs the air.
10 There seems no time to want a drink of water.
Nurse looks so far away. And here and there
Music and roses burst through crimson slaughter.
He can't remember where he saw blue sky . . .
The trench is narrower. Cold, he's cold; yet hot –
15 And there's no light to see the voices by . . .
There is no time to ask . . . he knows not what.

Disabled

He sat in a wheeled chair, waiting for dark,
And shivered in his ghastly suit of grey,
Legless, sewn short at elbow. Through the park
Voices of boys rang saddening like a hymn,
5 Voices of play and pleasure after day,
Till gathering sleep had mothered them from him.

* * *

About this time Town used to swing so gay
When glow-lamps budded in the light blue trees,
And girls glanced lovelier as the air grew dim, –
10 In the old times, before he threw away his knees.
Now he will never feel again how slim
Girls' waists are, or how warm their subtle hands.
All of them touch him like some queer disease.

* * *

There was an artist silly for his face,
15 For it was younger than his youth, last year.
Now, he is old; his back will never brace;
He's lost his colour very far from here,
Poured it down shell-holes till the veins ran dry,
And half his lifetime lapsed in the hot race
20 And leap of purple spurted from his thigh.

* * *

One time he liked a blood-smear down his leg,
After the matches, carried shoulder-high.
It was after football, when he'd drunk a peg,
He thought he'd better join. – He wonders why.
25 Someone had said he'd look a god in kilts,
That's why; and maybe, too, to please his Meg,
Aye, that was it, to please the giddy jilts
He asked to join. He didn't have to beg;
Smiling they wrote his lie: aged nineteen years.
30 Germans he scarcely thought of; all their guilt,
And Austria's, did not move him. And no fears
Of Fear came yet. He thought of jewelled hilts

For daggers in plaid socks; of smart salutes;
And care of arms; and leave; and pay arrears;
35 Esprit de corps; and hints for young recruits.
And soon, he was drafted out with drums and cheers.

* * *

Some cheered him home, but not as crowds cheer Goal.
Only a solemn man who brought him fruits
Thanked him; and then enquired about his soul.

* * *

40 Now, he will spend a few sick years in institutes,
And do what things the rules consider wise,
And take whatever pity they may dole.
Tonight he noticed how the women's eyes
Passed from him to the strong men that were whole.
45 How cold and late it is! Why don't they come
And put him into bed? Why don't they come?

Dulce et Decorum Est

Bent double, like old beggars under sacks,
Knock-kneed, coughing like hags, we cursed through sludge,
Till on the haunting flares we turned our backs
And towards our distant rest began to trudge.
5 Men marched asleep. Many had lost their boots
But limped on, blood-shod. All went lame; all blind;
Drunk with fatigue; deaf even to the hoots
Of tired, outstripped Five-Nines that dropped behind.

Gas! GAS! Quick, boys! – An ecstasy of fumbling,
10 Fitting the clumsy helmets just in time;
But someone still was yelling out and stumbling,
And flound'ring like a man in fire or lime . . .
Dim, through the misty panes and thick green light,
As under a green sea, I saw him drowning.

15 In all my dreams, before my helpless sight,
He plunges at me, guttering, choking, drowning.

If in some smothering dreams you too could pace
Behind the wagon that we flung him in,
And watch the white eyes writhing in his face,
20 His hanging face, like a devil's sick of sin;
If you could hear, at every jolt, the blood
Come gargling from the froth-corrupted lungs,
Obscene as cancer, bitter as the cud
Of vile, incurable sores on innocent tongues, –
25 My friend, you would not tell with such high zest
To children ardent for some desperate glory,
The old Lie: Dulce et decorum est
Pro patria mori.

Exposure

Our brains ache, in the merciless iced east winds that knive us . . .
Wearied we keep awake because the night is silent . . .
Low, drooping flares confuse our memory of the salient . . .
Worried by silence, sentries whisper, curious, nervous,
5   But nothing happens.

Watching, we hear the mad gusts tugging on the wire,
Like twitching agonies of men among its brambles.
Northward, incessantly, the flickering gunnery rumbles,
Far off, like a dull rumour of some other war.
10   What are we doing here?

The poignant misery of dawn begins to grow . . .
We only know war lasts, rain soaks, and clouds sag stormy.
Dawn massing in the east her melancholy army
Attacks once more in ranks on shivering ranks of grey,
15   But nothing happens.

Sudden successive flights of bullets streak the silence.
Less deathly than the air that shudders black with snow,
With sidelong flowing flakes that flock, pause, and renew;
We watch them wandering up and down the wind's nonchalance,
20   But nothing happens.

Pale flakes with fingering stealth come feeling for our faces –
We cringe in holes, back on forgotten dreams, and stare, snow-dazed,
Deep into grassier ditches. So we drowse, sun-dozed,
Littered with blossoms trickling where the blackbird fusses,
25   – Is it that we are dying?

Slowly our ghosts drag home: glimpsing the sunk fires, glozed
With crusted dark-red jewels; crickets jingle there;
For hours the innocent mice rejoice: the house is theirs;
Shutters and doors, all closed: on us the doors are closed, –
30   We turn back to our dying.

Since we believe not otherwise can kind fires burn;
Nor ever suns smile true on child, or field, or fruit.
For God's invincible spring our love is made afraid;
Therefore, not loath, we lie out here; therefore were born,
35   For love of God seems dying.

Tonight, this frost will fasten on this mud and us,
Shrivelling many hands, puckering foreheads crisp.
The burying-party, picks and shovels in shaking grasp,
Pause over half-known faces. All their eyes are ice,
40   But nothing happens.

Futility

Move him into the sun –
Gently its touch awoke him once,
At home, whispering of fields half-sown.
Always it woke him, even in France,
5 Until this morning and this snow.
If anything might rouse him now
The kind old sun will know.

Think how it wakes the seeds –
Woke once the clays of a cold star.
10 Are limbs, so dear achieved, are sides
Full-nerved, still warm, too hard to stir?
Was it for this the clay grew tall?
– O what made fatuous sunbeams toil
To break earth's sleep at all?

Inspection

'You! What d'you mean by this?' I rapped.
'You dare come on parade like this?'
'Please, sir, it's – ' ''Old yer mouth,' the sergeant snapped.
'I takes 'is name, sir?' – 'Please, and then dismiss.'

5 Some days 'confined to camp' he got,
For being 'dirty on parade'.
He told me, afterwards, the damnèd spot
Was blood, his own. 'Well, blood is dirt,' I said.

'Blood's dirt,' he laughed, looking away,
10 Far off to where his wound had bled
And almost merged for ever into clay.
'The world is washing out its stains,' he said.
'It doesn't like our cheeks so red:
Young blood's its great objection.
15 But when we're duly white-washed, being dead,
The race will bear Field Marshal God's inspection.'

Mental Cases

Who are these? Why sit they here in twilight?
Wherefore rock they, purgatorial shadows,
Drooping tongues from jaws that slob their relish,
Baring teeth that leer like skulls' teeth wicked?
5 Stroke on stroke of pain, – but what slow panic,
Gouged these chasms round their fretted sockets?
Ever from their hair and through their hands' palms
Misery swelters. Surely we have perished
Sleeping, and walk hell; but who these hellish?

10 – These are men whose minds the Dead have ravished.
Memory fingers in their hair of murders,
Multitudinous murders they once witnessed.
Wading sloughs of flesh these helpless wander,
Treading blood from lungs that had loved laughter.
15 Always they must see these things and hear them,
Batter of guns and shatter of flying muscles,
Carnage incomparable, and human squander
Rucked too thick for these men's extrication.

Therefore still their eyeballs shrink tormented
20 Back into their brains, because on their sense
Sunlight seems a blood-smear; night comes blood-black;
Dawn breaks open like a wound that bleeds afresh.
– Thus their heads wear this hilarious, hideous,
Awful falseness of set-smiling corpses.
25 – Thus their hands are plucking at each other;
Picking at the rope-knouts of their scourging;
Snatching after us who smote them, brother,
Pawing us who dealt them war and madness.

Spring Offensive

Halted against the shade of a last hill
They fed, and eased of pack-loads, were at ease;
And leaning on the nearest chest or knees
Carelessly slept.
                        But many there stood still
5 To face the stark blank sky beyond the ridge,
Knowing their feet had come to the end of the world.
Marvelling they stood, and watched the long grass swirled
By the May breeze, murmurous with wasp and midge;
And though the summer oozed into their veins
10 Like an injected drug for their bodies' pains,
Sharp on their souls hung the imminent ridge of grass,
Fearfully flashed the sky's mysterious glass.

Hour after hour they ponder the warm field
And the far valley behind, where buttercups
15 Had blessed with gold their slow boots coming up;
When even the little brambles would not yield
But clutched and clung to them like sorrowing arms.
They breathe like trees unstirred.

Till like a cold gust thrills the little word
20 At which each body and its soul begird
And tighten them for battle. No alarms
Of bugles, no high flags, no clamorous haste, –
Only a lift and flare of eyes that faced
The sun, like a friend with whom their love is done.
25 O larger shone that smile against the sun, –
Mightier than his whose bounty these have spurned.

So, soon they topped the hill, and raced together
Over an open stretch of herb and heather
Exposed. And instantly the whole sky burned
30 With fury against them; earth set sudden cups
In thousands for their blood; and the green slope
Chasmed and deepened sheer to infinite space.

Of them who running on that last high place
Breasted the surf of bullets, or went up
35 On the hot blast and fury of hell's upsurge,
Or plunged and fell away past this world's verge,
Some say God caught them even before they fell.

But what say such as from existence' brink
Ventured but drave too swift to sink,
40 The few who rushed in the body to enter hell,
And there out-fiending all its fiends and flames
With superhuman inhumanities,
Long-famous glories, immemorial shames –
And crawling slowly back, have by degrees
45 Regained cool peaceful air in wonder –
Why speak not they of comrades that went under?

Strange Meeting

It seemed that out of battle I escaped
Down some profound dull tunnel, long since scooped
Through granites which titanic wars had groined.

Yet also there encumbered sleepers groaned,
5 Too fast in thought or death to be bestirred.
Then, as I probed them, one sprang up, and stared
With piteous recognition in fixed eyes,
Lifting distressful hands, as if to bless.
And by his smile, I knew that sullen hall, –
10 By his dead smile I knew we stood in Hell.

With a thousand pains that vision's face was grained;
Yet no blood reached there from the upper ground,
And no guns thumped, or down the flues made moan.
'Strange friend,' I said, 'here is no cause to mourn.'
15 'None,' said that other, 'save the undone years,
The hopelessness. Whatever hope is yours,
Was my life also; I went hunting wild
After the wildest beauty in the world,
Which lies not calm in eyes, or braided hair,
20 But mocks the steady running of the hour,
And if it grieves, grieves richlier than here.
For by my glee might many men have laughed,
And of my weeping something had been left,
Which must die now. I mean the truth untold,
25 The pity of war, the pity war distilled.
Now men will go content with what we spoiled,
Or, discontent, boil bloody, and be spilled.
They will be swift with swiftness of the tigress.
None will break ranks, though nations trek from progress.
30 Courage was mine, and I had mystery,
Wisdom was mine, and I had mastery:
To miss the march of this retreating world
Into vain citadels that are not walled.

Then, when much blood had clogged their chariot-wheels,
35 I would go up and wash them from sweet wells,
Even with truths that lie too deep for taint.
I would have poured my spirit without stint
But not through wounds; not on the cess of war.
Foreheads of men have bled where no wounds were.

40 'I am the enemy you killed, my friend.
I knew you in this dark: for so you frowned
Yesterday through me as you jabbed and killed.
I parried; but my hands were loath and cold.
Let us sleep now . . . '

The Chances

I 'mind as how the night before that show
Us five got talkin'; we was in the know.
'Ah well,' says Jimmy, and he's seen some scrappin',
'There ain't no more than five things as can happen, –
5 You get knocked out; else wounded, bad or cushy;
Scuppered; or nowt except you're feelin' mushy.'

One of us got the knock-out, blown to chops;
One lad was hurt, like, losin' both his props;
And one – to use the word of hypocrites –
10 Had the misfortune to be took by Fritz.
Now me, I wasn't scratched, praise God Almighty,
Though next time please I'll thank Him for a blighty.
But poor old Jim, he's livin' and he's not;
He reckoned he'd five chances, and he had:
15 He's wounded, killed, and pris'ner, all the lot,
The flamin' lot all rolled in one. Jim's mad.

The Letter

With B.E.F. June 10. Dear Wife,
(Oh blast this pencil. 'Ere, Bill, lend's a knife.)
I'm in the pink at present, dear.
I think the war will end this year.
5 We don't see much of them square-'eaded 'Uns.
We're out of harm's way, not bad fed.
I'm longing for a taste of your old buns.
(Say, Jimmie, spare's a bite of bread.)
There don't seem much to say just now.
10 (Yer what? Then don't, yer ruddy cow!
And give us back me cigarette!)
I'll soon be 'ome. You mustn't fret.
My feet's improvin', as I told you of.
We're out in rest now. Never fear.
15 (VRACH! By crumbs, but that was near.)
Mother might spare you half a sov.
Kiss Nell and Bert. When me and you –
(Eh? What the 'ell! Stand to? Stand to!
Jim, give's a hand with pack on, lad.
20 Guh! Christ! I'm hit. Take 'old. Aye, bad.
No damn your iodine. Jim? 'Ere!
Write my old girl, Jim, there's a dear.)

The Dead-Beat

He dropped, – more sullenly than wearily,
Lay stupid like a cod, heavy like meat,
And none of us could kick him to his feet;
– Just blinked at my revolver, blearily;
5   – Didn't appear to know a war was on,
Or see the blasted trench at which he stared.
'I'll do 'em in,' he whined. 'If this hand's spared,
I'll murder them, I will.'

                    A low voice said,
'It's Blighty, p'raps, he sees; his pluck's all gone,
10 Dreaming of all the valiant, that *aren't* dead:
Bold uncles, smiling ministerially;
Maybe his brave young wife, getting her fun
In some new home, improved materially.
It's not these stiffs have crazed him; nor the Hun.'

15 We sent him down at last, out of the way.
Unwounded; – stout lad, too, before that strafe.
Malingering? Stretcher-bearers winked, 'Not half!'

Next day I heard the Doc's well-whiskied laugh:
'That scum you sent last night soon died. Hooray!'

The Send-Off

Down the close darkening lanes they sang their way
To the siding-shed,
And lined the train with faces grimly gay.

Their breasts were stuck all white with wreath and spray
5 As men's are, dead.

Dull porters watched them, and a casual tramp
Stood staring hard,
Sorry to miss them from the upland camp.

Then, unmoved, signals nodded, and a lamp
10 Winked to the guard.

So secretly, like wrongs hushed-up, they went.
They were not ours:
We never heard to which front these were sent;

Nor there if they yet mock what women meant
15 Who gave them flowers.

Shall they return to beating of great bells
In wild train-loads?
A few, a few, too few for drums and yells,

May creep back, silent, to village wells,
20 Up half-known roads.

The Sentry

We'd found an old Boche dug-out, and he knew,
And gave us hell; for shell on frantic shell
Lit full on top, but never quite burst through.
Rain, guttering down in waterfalls of slime,
5 Kept slush waist-high and rising hour by hour,
And choked the steps too thick with clay to climb.
What murk of air remained stank old, and sour
With fumes from whizz-bangs, and the smell of men
Who'd lived there years, and left their curse in the den,
10 If not their corpses . . .
                    There we herded from the blast
Of whizz-bangs; but one found our door at last, –
Buffeting eyes and breath, snuffing the candles,
And thud! flump! thud! down the steep steps came thumping
And sploshing in the flood, deluging muck, –
15 The sentry's body; then his rifle, handles
Of old Boche bombs, and mud in ruck on ruck.
We dredged it up, for dead, until he whined,
'O sir – my eyes, – I'm blind, – I'm blind, – I'm blind.'
Coaxing, I held a flame against his lids
20 And said if he could see the least blurred light
He was not blind; in time they'd get all right.
'I can't,' he sobbed. Eyeballs, huge-bulged like squids',
Watch my dreams still, – yet I forgot him there
In posting Next for duty, and sending a scout
25 To beg a stretcher somewhere, and flound'ring about
To other posts under the shrieking air.

Those other wretches, how they bled and spewed,
And one who would have drowned himself for good, –
I try not to remember these things now.
30 Let Dread hark back for one word only: how,
Half-listening to that sentry's moans and jumps,
And the wild chattering of his shivered teeth,
Renewed most horribly whenever crumps
Pummelled the roof and slogged the air beneath, –
35 Through the dense din, I say, we heard him shout
'I see your lights!' – But ours had long gone out.

Christina Rossetti

A Dumb Friend

I planted a young tree when I was young;
　　But now the tree is grown and I am old:
　　There wintry robin shelters from the cold
　　　　And tunes his silver tongue.

5　A green and living tree I planted it,
　　A glossy-foliaged tree of evergreen:
　　All thro' the noontide heat it spread a screen
　　　　Whereunder I might sit.

But now I only watch it where it towers:
10　　I, sitting at my window, watch it tossed
　　By rattling gale, or silvered by the frost;
　　　　Or, when sweet summer flowers,

Wagging its round green head with stately grace
　　In tender winds that kiss it and go by:
15　　It shows a green full age; and what show I?
　　　　A faded wrinkled face.

So often have I watched it, till mine eyes
　　Have filled with tears and I have ceased to see;
　　That now it seems a very friend to me
20　　　　In all my secrets wise.

A faithful pleasant friend, who year by year
　　Grew with my growth and strengthened with my strength,
　　But whose green lifetime shows a longer length:
　　　　When I shall not sit here

25　It still will bud in spring, and shed rare leaves
　　In autumn, and in summer heat give shade,
　　And warmth in winter; when my bed is made
　　　　In shade the cypress weaves.

An Apple-Gathering

I plucked pink blossoms from mine apple tree
   And wore them all that evening in my hair:
Then in due season when I went to see
    I found no apples there.

5 With dangling basket all along the grass
    As I had come I went the selfsame track:
My neighbours mocked me while they saw me pass
    So empty-handed back.

Lilian and Lilias smiled in trudging by,
10   Their heaped-up basket teazed me like a jeer;
Sweet-voiced they sang beneath the sunset sky,
    Their mother's home was near.

Plump Gertrude passed me with her basket full,
    A stronger hand than hers helped it along;
15 A voice talked with her thro' the shadows cool
    More sweet to me than song.

Ah Willie, Willie, was my love less worth
    Than apples with their green leaves piled above?
I counted rosiest apples on the earth
20   Of far less worth than love.

So once it was with me you stooped to talk
    Laughing and listening in this very lane:
To think that by this way we used to walk
    We shall not walk again!

25 I let my neighbours pass me, ones and twos
    And groups; the latest said the night grew chill,
And hastened: but I loitered, while the dews
    Fell fast I loitered still.

Cousin Kate

I was a cottage maiden
  Hardened by sun and air,
Contented with my cottage mates,
  Not mindful I was fair.
5 Why did a great lord find me out,
  And praise my flaxen hair?
Why did a great lord find me out
  To fill my heart with care?

He lured me to his palace home—
10   Woe's me for joy thereof—
To lead a shameless shameful life,
  His plaything and his love.
He wore me like a silken knot,
  He changed me like a glove;
15 So now I moan, an unclean thing,
  Who might have been a dove.

O Lady Kate, my cousin Kate,
  You grew more fair than I:
He saw you at your father's gate,
20   Chose you, and cast me by.
He watched your steps along the lane,
  Your work among the rye;
He lifted you from mean estate
  To sit with him on high.

25 Because you were so good and pure
  He bound you with his ring:
The neighbours call you good and pure,
  Call me an outcast thing.
Even so I sit and howl in dust,
30   You sit in gold and sing:
Now which of us has tenderer heart?
  You had the stronger wing.

O cousin Kate, my love was true,
  Your love was writ in sand:
35 If he had fooled not me but you,
  If you stood where I stand,
He'd not have won me with his love
  Nor bought me with his land;
I would have spit into his face
40   And not have taken his hand.

Yet I've a gift you have not got,
  And seem not like to get:
For all your clothes and wedding-ring
  I've little doubt you fret.
45 My fair-haired son, my shame, my pride,
  Cling closer, closer yet:
Your father would give lands for one
  To wear his coronet.

In an Artist's Studio

One face looks out from all his canvasses,
    One selfsame figure sits or walks or leans;
    We found her hidden just behind those screens,
That mirror gave back all her loveliness.
5 A queen in opal or in ruby dress,
    A nameless girl in freshest summer greens,
    A saint, an angel;—every canvass means
The same one meaning, neither more nor less.
He feeds upon her face by day and night,
10   And she with true kind eyes looks back on him
Fair as the moon and joyful as the light:
    Not wan with waiting, not with sorrow dim;
Not as she is, but was when hope shone bright;
    Not as she is, but as she fills his dream.

In the Willow Shade

I sat beneath a willow tree,
    Where water falls and calls;
While fancies upon fancies solaced me,
    Some true, and some were false.

5 Who set their heart upon a hope
    That never comes to pass,
Droop in the end like fading heliotrope
    The sun's wan looking-glass.

Who set their will upon a whim
10   Clung to thro' good and ill,
Are wrecked alike whether they sink or swim,
    Or hit or miss their will.

All things are vain that wax and wane,
    For which we waste our breath;
15 Love only doth not wane and is not vain,
    Love only outlives death.

A singing lark rose toward the sky,
    Circling he sang amain;
He sang, a speck scarce visible sky-high,
20   And then he sank again.

A second like a sunlit spark
    Flashed singing up his track;
But never overtook that foremost lark,
    And songless fluttered back.

25 A hovering melody of birds
    Haunted the air above;
They clearly sang contentment without words,
    And youth and joy and love.

O silvery weeping willow tree
30   With all leaves shivering,
Have you no purpose but to shadow me
    Beside this rippled spring?

On this first fleeting day of Spring,
    For Winter is gone by,
35 And every bird on every quivering wing
    Floats in a sunny sky;

On this first Summer-like soft day,
    While sunshine steeps the air,
And every cloud has gat itself away,
40   And birds sing everywhere.

Have you no purpose in the world
    But thus to shadow me
With all your tender drooping twigs unfurled,
    O weeping willow tree?

45 With all your tremulous leaves outspread
    Betwixt me and the sun,
While here I loiter on a mossy bed
    With half my work undone;

My work undone, that should be done
50   At once with all my might;
For after the long day and lingering sun
    Comes the unworking night.

This day is lapsing on its way,
    Is lapsing out of sight;
55 And after all the chances of the day
    Comes the resourceless night.

The weeping willow shook its head
    And stretched its shadow long;
The west grew crimson, the sun smouldered red,
60   The birds forbore a song.

Slow wind sighed thro' the willow leaves,
    The ripple made a moan,
The world drooped murmuring like a thing that grieves;
    And then I felt alone.

65 I rose to go, and felt the chill,
    And shivered as I went;
Yet shivering wondered, and I wonder still,
    What more that willow meant;

That silvery weeping willow tree
70   With all leaves shivering,
Which spent one long day overshadowing me
    Beside a spring in Spring.

Maude Clare

Out of the church she followed them
    With a lofty step and mien:
His bride was like a village maid,
    Maude Clare was like a queen.

5 "Son Thomas," his lady mother said,
    With smiles, almost with tears:
"May Nell and you but live as true
    As we have done for years;

"Your father thirty years ago
10   Had just your tale to tell;
But he was not so pale as you,
    Nor I so pale as Nell."

My lord was pale with inward strife,
    And Nell was pale with pride;
15 My lord gazed long on pale Maude Clare
    Or ever he kissed the bride.

"Lo, I have brought my gift, my lord,
    Have brought my gift," she said:
"To bless the hearth, to bless the board,
20   To bless the marriage-bed.

"Here's my half of the golden chain
    You wore about your neck,
That day we waded ankle-deep
    For lilies in the beck:

25 "Here's my half of the faded leaves
    We plucked from budding bough,
With feet amongst the lily leaves,—
    The lilies are budding now."

He strove to match her scorn with scorn,
30   He faltered in his place:
"Lady," he said,—"Maude Clare," he said—
    "Maude Clare:"—and hid his face.

She turn'd to Nell: "My Lady Nell,
    I have a gift for you;
35 Tho', were it fruit, the bloom were gone,
    Or, were it flowers, the dew.

"Take my share of a fickle heart,
    Mine of a paltry love:
Take it or leave it as you will,
40   I wash my hands thereof."

"And what you leave," said Nell, "I'll take,
    And what you spurn, I'll wear;
For he's my lord for better and worse,
    And him I love, Maude Clare.

45 "Yea, tho' you're taller by the head,
    More wise, and much more fair;
I'll love him till he loves me best,
    Me best of all, Maude Clare."

"No, Thank You, John"

I never said I loved you, John:
   Why will you teaze me day by day,
And wax a weariness to think upon
   With always "do" and "pray"?

5 You know I never loved you, John;
   No fault of mine made me your toast:
Why will you haunt me with a face as wan
   As shows an hour-old ghost?

I dare say Meg or Moll would take
10   Pity upon you, if you'd ask:
And pray don't remain single for my sake
   Who can't perform that task.

I have no heart?—Perhaps I have not;
   But then you're mad to take offence
15 That I don't give you what I have not got:
   Use your own common sense.

Let bygones be bygones:
   Don't call me false, who owed not to be true:
I'd rather answer "No" to fifty Johns
20   Than answer "Yes" to you.

Let's mar our pleasant days no more,
   Song-birds of passage, days of youth:
Catch at today, forget the days before:
   I'll wink at your untruth.

25 Let us strike hands as hearty friends;
   No more, no less; and friendship's good:
Only don't keep in view ulterior ends,
   And points not understood

In open treaty. Rise above
30   Quibbles and shuffling off and on:
Here's friendship for you if you like; but love,—
   No, thank you, John.

Promises Like Piecrust

Promise me no promises,
    So will I not promise you;
Keep we both our liberties,
    Never false and never true:
5 Let us hold the die uncast,
    Free to come as free to go;
For I cannot know your past,
    And of mine what can you know?

You, so warm, may once have been
10   Warmer towards another one;
I, so cold, may once have seen
    Sunlight, once have felt the sun:
Who shall show us if it was
    Thus indeed in time of old?
15 Fades the image from the glass
    And the fortune is not told.

If you promised, you might grieve
    For lost liberty again;
If I promised, I believe
20   I should fret to break the chain:
Let us be the friends we were,
    Nothing more but nothing less;
Many thrive on frugal fare
    Who would perish of excess.

Remember

Remember me when I am gone away,
    Gone far away into the silent land;
    When you can no more hold me by the hand,
Nor I half turn to go yet turning stay.
5 Remember me when no more day by day
    You tell me of our future that you planned:
    Only remember me; you understand
It will be late to counsel then or pray.
Yet if you should forget me for a while
10   And afterwards remember, do not grieve:
    For if the darkness and corruption leave
    A vestige of the thoughts that once I had,
Better by far you should forget and smile
    Than that you should remember and be sad.

On the Wing

Once in a dream (for once I dreamed of you)
    We stood together in an open field;
    Above our heads two swift-winged pigeons wheeled,
Sporting at ease and courting full in view.
5 When loftier still a broadening darkness flew,
    Down-swooping, and a ravenous hawk revealed;
    Too weak to fight, too fond to fly, they yield;
So farewell life and love and pleasures new.
Then as their plumes fell fluttering to the ground,
10   Their snow-white plumage flecked with crimson drops,
      I wept, and thought I turned towards you to weep:
    But you were gone; while rustling hedgerow tops
Bent in a wind which bore to me a sound
    Of far-off piteous bleat of lambs and sheep.

Shut Out

The door was shut. I looked between
   Its iron bars; and saw it lie,
   My garden, mine, beneath the sky,
Pied with all flowers bedewed and green:

5 From bough to bough the song-birds crossed,
   From flower to flower the moths and bees;
   With all its nests and stately trees
It had been mine, and it was lost.

A shadowless spirit kept the gate,
10   Blank and unchanging like the grave.
   I peering thro' said: "Let me have
Some buds to cheer my outcast state."

He answered not. "Or give me, then,
   But one small twig from shrub or tree;
15   And bid my home remember me
Until I come to it again."

The spirit was silent; but he took
   Mortar and stone to build a wall;
   He left no loophole great or small
20 Thro' which my straining eyes might look:

So now I sit here quite alone
   Blinded with tears; nor grieve for that,
   For nought is left worth looking at
Since my delightful land is gone.

25 A violet bed is budding near,
   Wherein a lark has made her nest:
   And good they are, but not the best;
And dear they are, but not so dear.

Spring Quiet

Gone were but the Winter,
   Come were but the Spring,
I would go to a covert
   Where the birds sing;

5 Where in the whitethorn
   Singeth the thrush,
And a robin sings
   In the holly-bush.

Full of fresh scents
10   Are the budding boughs
Arching high over
   A cool green house:

Full of sweet scents,
   And whispering air
15 Which sayeth softly:
   "We spread no snare;

"Here dwell in safety,
   Here dwell alone,
With a clear stream
20   And a mossy stone.

"Here the sun shineth
   Most shadily;
Here is heard an echo
   Of the far sea,
25   Tho' far off it be."

Symbols

I watched a rosebud very long
    Brought on by dew and sun and shower,
    Waiting to see the perfect flower:
Then, when I thought it should be strong,
5   It opened at the matin hour
       And fell at evensong.

I watched a nest from day to day,
    A green nest full of pleasant shade,
    Wherein three speckled eggs were laid:
10 But when they should have hatched in May,
    The two old birds had grown afraid
      Or tired, and flew away.

Then in my wrath I broke the bough
    That I had tended so with care,
15   Hoping its scent should fill the air;
I crushed the eggs, not heeding how
    Their ancient promise had been fair:
      I would have vengeance now.

But the dead branch spoke from the sod,
20   And the eggs answered me again:
    Because we failed dost thou complain?
Is thy wrath just? And what if God,
    Who waiteth for thy fruits in vain,
      Should also take the rod?

The Key-Note

Where are the songs I used to know,
    Where are the notes I used to sing?
    I have forgotten everything
I used to know so long ago;
5 Summer has followed after Spring;
    Now Autumn is so shrunk and sere,
I scarcely think a sadder thing
    Can be the Winter of my year.

Yet Robin sings thro' Winter's rest,
10   When bushes put their berries on;
    While they their ruddy jewels don,
He sings out of a ruddy breast;
The hips and haws and ruddy breast
    Make one spot warm where snowflakes lie,
15 They break and cheer the unlovely rest
    Of Winter's pause—and why not I?

The World

By day she woos me, soft, exceeding fair:
    But all night as the moon so changeth she;
    Loathsome and foul with hideous leprosy
And subtle serpents gliding in her hair.
5 By day she woos me to the outer air,
    Ripe fruits, sweet flowers, and full satiety:
    But thro' the night, a beast she grins at me,
A very monster void of love and prayer.
By day she stands a lie: by night she stands
10   In all the naked horror of the truth
With pushing horns and clawed and clutching hands.
Is this a friend indeed; that I should sell
    My soul to her, give her my life and youth,
Till my feet, cloven too, take hold on hell?

William Shakespeare

Sonnet 2

When forty winters shall besiege thy brow,
And dig deep trenches in thy beauty's field,
Thy youth's proud livery so gazed on now
Will be a tattered weed of small worth held:
5 Then, being asked where all thy beauty lies,
Where all the treasure of thy lusty days,
To say within thine own deep-sunken eyes
Were an all-eating shame, and thriftless praise.
How much more praise deserved thy beauty's use
10 If thou couldst answer 'This fair child of mine
Shall sum my count, and make my old excuse',
Proving his beauty by succession thine.
　　This were to be new made when thou art old,
　　And see thy blood warm when thou feel'st it cold.

Sonnet 3

Look in thy glass and tell the face thou viewest
Now is the time that face should form another,
Whose fresh repair if now thou not renewest
Thou dost beguile the world, unbless some mother.
5 For where is she so fair whose uneared womb
Disdains the tillage of thy husbandry?
Or who is he so fond will be the tomb
Of his self-love to stop posterity?
Thou art thy mother's glass, and she in thee
10 Calls back the lovely April of her prime;
So thou through windows of thine age shalt see,
Despite of wrinkles, this thy golden time.
　　But if thou live rememb'red not to be,
　　Die single, and thine image dies with thee.

Sonnet 15

When I consider every thing that grows
Holds in perfection but a little moment;
That this huge stage presenteth naught but shows,
Whereon the stars in secret influence comment;
5 When I perceive that men as plants increase,
Cheerèd and checked even by the selfsame sky,
Vaunt in their youthful sap, at height decrease,
And wear their brave state out of memory;
Then the conceit of this inconstant stay
10 Sets you most rich in youth before my sight,
Where wasteful time debateth with decay
To change your day of youth to sullied night,
    And, all in war with Time for love of you,
    As he takes from you, I engraft you new.

Sonnet 18

Shall I compare thee to a summer's day?
Thou art more lovely and more temperate:
Rough winds do shake the darling buds of May,
And summer's lease hath all too short a date;
5 Sometime too hot the eye of heaven shines,
And often is his gold complexion dimmed,
And every fair from fair sometime declines,
By chance or nature's changing course untrimmed:
But thy eternal summer shall not fade,
10 Nor lose possession of that fair thou ow'st;
Nor shall Death brag thou wand'rest in his shade,
When in eternal lines to time thou grow'st.
    So long as men can breathe or eyes can see,
    So long lives this, and this gives life to thee.

Sonnet 19

Devouring Time, blunt thou the lion's paws,
And make the earth devour her own sweet brood,
Pluck the keen teeth from the fierce tiger's jaws,
And burn the long-lived phoenix in her blood,
5 Make glad and sorry seasons as thou fleet'st,
And do whate'er thou wilt, swift-footed Time,
To the wide world and all her fading sweets:
But I forbid thee one most heinous crime,
O carve not with thy hours my love's fair brow,
10 Nor draw no lines there with thine antique pen.
Him in thy course untainted do allow
For beauty's pattern to succeeding men.
    Yet do thy worst, old Time: despite thy wrong,
    My love shall in my verse ever live young.

Sonnet 34

Why didst thou promise such a beauteous day,
And make me travel forth without my cloak,
To let base clouds o'ertake me in my way,
Hiding thy brav'ry in their rotten smoke?
5 'Tis not enough that through the cloud thou break
To dry the rain on my storm-beaten face,
For no man well of such a salve can speak
That heals the wound and cures not the disgrace;
Nor can thy shame give physic to my grief:
10 Though thou repent, yet I have still the loss.
Th' offender's sorrow lends but weak relief
To him that bears the strong offence's cross.
    Ah, but those tears are pearl which thy love sheds,
    And they are rich, and ransom all ill deeds.

Sonnet 43

When most I wink, then do mine eyes best see,
For all the day they view things unrespected,
But when I sleep, in dreams they look on thee,
And, darkly bright, are bright in dark directed.
5 Then thou, whose shadow shadows doth make bright,
How would thy shadow's form form happy show,
To the clear day with thy much clearer light,
When to unseeing eyes thy shade shines so?
How would (I say) mine eyes be blessèd made
10 By looking on thee in the living day,
When in dead night thy fair imperfect shade
Through heavy sleep on sightless eyes doth stay?
    All days are nights to see till I see thee,
    And nights bright days when dreams do show thee me.

Sonnet 56

Sweet love, renew thy force. Be it not said
Thy edge should blunter be than appetite,
Which but today by feeding is allayed,
Tomorrow sharpened in his former might.
5 So love be thou, although today thou fill
Thy hungry eyes, even till they wink with fullness,
Tomorrow see again, and do not kill
The spirit of love with a perpetual dullness.
Let this sad int'rim like the ocean be,
10 Which parts the shore where two, contracted new,
Come daily to the banks, that when they see
Return of love, more blest may be the view;
    Or call it winter, which being full of care,
    Makes summer's welcome thrice more wished, more rare.

Sonnet 65

Since brass, nor stone, nor earth, nor boundless sea,
But sad mortality o'ersways their power,
How with this rage shall beauty hold a plea,
Whose action is no stronger than a flower?
5 O how shall summer's honey breath hold out
Against the wrackful siege of batt'ring days,
When rocks impregnable are not so stout,
Nor gates of steel so strong, but time decays?
O fearful meditation; where, alack,
10 Shall Time's best jewel from Time's chest lie hid?
Or what strong hand can hold his swift foot back,
Or who his spoil of beauty can forbid?
    O none, unless this miracle have might,
    That in black ink my love may still shine bright.

Sonnet 73

That time of year thou mayst in me behold
When yellow leaves, or none, or few, do hang
Upon those boughs which shake against the cold,
Bare ruined choirs, where late the sweet birds sang.
5 In me thou seest the twilight of such day
As after sunset fadeth in the west,
Which by and by black night doth take away,
Death's second self, that seals up all in rest.
In me thou seest the glowing of such fire
10 That on the ashes of his youth doth lie,
As the death-bed whereon it must expire,
Consumed with that which it was nourished by.
    This thou perceiv'st, which makes thy love more strong,
    To love that well, which thou must leave ere long.

Sonnet 81

Or I shall live your epitaph to make,
Or you survive when I in earth am rotten,
From hence your memory death cannot take,
Although in me each part will be forgotten.
5 Your name from hence immortal life shall have,
Though I (once gone) to all the world must die.
The earth can yield me but a common grave
When you entombèd in men's eyes shall lie:
Your monument shall be my gentle verse,
10 Which eyes not yet created shall o'er-read,
And tongues-to-be your being shall rehearse,
When all the breathers of this world are dead.
      You still shall live (such virtue hath my pen)
      Where breath most breathes, even in the mouths of men.

Sonnet 116

Let me not to the marriage of true minds
Admit impediments; love is not love
Which alters when it alteration finds,
Or bends with the remover to remove.
5 O no, it is an ever-fixèd mark,
That looks on tempests and is never shaken;
It is the star to every wandering barque,
Whose worth's unknown, although his height be taken.
Love's not Time's fool, though rosy lips and cheeks
10 Within his bending sickle's compass come.
Love alters not with his brief hours and weeks,
But bears it out even to the edge of doom.
      If this be error and upon me proved,
      I never writ, nor no man ever loved.

Sonnet 129

Th' expense of spirit in a waste of shame
Is lust in action, and, till action, lust
Is perjured, murd'rous, bloody, full of blame,
Savage, extreme, rude, cruel, not to trust,
5 Enjoyed no sooner but despisèd straight,
Past reason hunted, and, no sooner had,
Past reason hated as a swallowed bait
On purpose laid to make the taker mad,
Mad in pursuit, and in possession so,
10 Had, having, and in quest to have, extreme,
A bliss in proof and proved a very woe,
Before, a joy proposed; behind, a dream.
    All this the world well knows, yet none knows well
    To shun the heaven that leads men to this hell.

Sonnet 130

My mistress' eyes are nothing like the sun,
Coral is far more red than her lips' red;
If snow be white, why then her breasts are dun;
If hairs be wires, black wires grow on her head.
5 I have seen roses damasked, red and white,
But no such roses see I in her cheeks,
And in some perfumes is there more delight
Than in the breath that from my mistress reeks.
I love to hear her speak, yet well I know
10 That music hath a far more pleasing sound.
I grant I never saw a goddess go:
My mistress when she walks treads on the ground.
    And yet, by heaven, I think my love as rare
    As any she belied with false compare.

Sonnet 147

My love is as a fever, longing still
For that which longer nurseth the disease,
Feeding on that which doth preserve the ill,
Th' uncertain sickly appetite to please.
5 My reason, the physician to my love,
Angry that his prescriptions are not kept,
Hath left me, and I desperate now approve
Desire is death, which physic did except.
Past cure I am, now Reason is past care,
10 And, frantic-mad with evermore unrest,
My thoughts and my discourse as madmen's are,
At random from the truth, vainly expressed.
  For I have sworn thee fair, and thought thee bright,
  Who art as black as hell, as dark as night.

Contemporary Poetry

Simon Armitage

About His Person

Five pounds fifty in change, exactly,
a library card on its date of expiry.

A postcard, stamped,
unwritten, but franked,

5   a pocket-size diary slashed with a pencil
from March twenty-fourth to the first of April.

A brace of keys for a mortise lock,
an analogue watch, self-winding, stopped.

A final demand
10 in his own hand,

a rolled-up note of explanation
planted there like a spray carnation

but beheaded, in his fist.
A shopping list.

15 A giveaway photograph stashed in his wallet,
a keepsake banked in the heart of a locket.

No gold or silver,
but crowning one finger

a ring of white unweathered skin.
20 That was everything.

Alaska

So you upped
and went. Big deal!
Now you must be sitting pretty.
Now you must see me
5 like a big kodiak bear,

safe and holed up
for the close season, then rumbled.
Girl, you must see me
like the crown prince
10 rattling

round his icy palace,
the cook and bottle-washer gone,
snuck off, a moonlight flit
to the next estate
15 for sick pay, wages, running water

in their own chambers, that type
of concession. Girl,
you must picture me: clueless,
the brand of a steam iron
20 on my dress shirt,

the fire left on all night,
the kitchen a scrap heap
of ring-pulls and beer cans
but let me say, girl,
25 the only time I came within a mile

of missing you
was a rainy Wednesday, April,
hauling in the sheets,
trying to handle
30 that big king-sizer. Girl,

you should see yourself with him,
out in the snowfield
like nodding donkeys
or further west, you and him,
35 hand in hand,

his and hers,
and all this
under my nose,
like the Bering Strait,
40 just a stone's throw away.

Gooseberry Season

Which reminds me. He appeared
at noon, asking for water. He'd walked from town
after losing his job, leaving a note for his wife and his brother
and locking his dog in the coal bunker.
5 We made him a bed

and he slept till Monday.
A week went by and he hung up his coat.
Then a month, and not a stroke of work, a word of thanks,
a farthing of rent or a sign of him leaving.
10 One evening he mentioned a recipe

for smooth, seedless gooseberry sorbet
but by then I was tired of him: taking pocket money
from my boy at cards, sucking up to my wife and on his last night
sizing up my daughter. He was smoking my pipe
15 as we stirred his supper.

Where does the hand become the wrist?
Where does the neck become the shoulder? The watershed
and then the weight, whatever turns up and tips us over that
    razor's edge
between something and nothing, between
20 one and the other.

I could have told him this
but didn't bother. We ran him a bath
and held him under, dried him off and dressed him
and loaded him into the back of the pick-up.
25 Then we drove without headlights

to the county boundary,
dropped the tailgate, and after my boy
had been through his pockets we dragged him like a mattress
across the meadow and on the count of four
30 threw him over the border.

This is not general knowledge, except
in gooseberry season, which reminds me, and at the table
I have been known to raise an eyebrow, or scoop the sorbet
into five equal portions, for the hell of it.
35 I mention this for a good reason.

Hitcher

I'd been tired, under
the weather, but the ansaphone kept screaming:
One more sick-note, mister, and you're finished. Fired.
I thumbed a lift to where the car was parked.
5 A Vauxhall Astra. It was hired.

I picked him up in Leeds.
He was following the sun to west from east
with just a toothbrush and the good earth for a bed. The truth,
he said, was blowin' in the wind,
10 or round the next bend.

I let him have it
on the top road out of Harrogate – once
with the head, then six times with the krooklok
in the face – and didn't even swerve.
15 I dropped it into third

and leant across
to let him out, and saw him in the mirror
bouncing off the kerb, then disappearing down the verge.
We were the same age, give or take a week.
20 He'd said he liked the breeze

to run its fingers
through his hair. It was twelve noon.
The outlook for the day was moderate to fair.
Stitch that, I remember thinking,
25 you can walk from there.

In Our Tenth Year

This book, this page, this harebell laid to rest
between these sheets, these leaves, if pressed still bleeds
a watercolour of the way we were.

Those years: the fuss of such and such a day,
5   that disagreement and its final word,
your inventory of names and dates and times,
my infantries of tall, dark, handsome lies.

A decade on, now we astound ourselves;
still two, still twinned but doubled now with love
10 and for a single night apart, alone,
how sure we are, each of the other half.

This harebell holds its own. Let's give it now
in air, with light, the chance to fade, to fold.
Here, take it from my hand. Now, let it go.

Kid

Batman, big shot, when you gave the order
to grow up, then let me loose to wander
leeward, freely through the wild blue yonder
as you liked to say, or ditched me, rather,
5 in the gutter . . . well, I turned the corner.
Now I've scotched that 'he was like a father
to me' rumour, sacked it, blown the cover
on that 'he was like an elder brother'
story, let the cat out on that caper
10 with the married woman, how you took her
downtown on expenses in the motor.
Holy robin-redbreast-nest-egg-shocker!
Holy roll-me-over-in-the-clover,
I'm not playing ball boy any longer
15 Batman, now I've doffed that off-the-shoulder
Sherwood-Forest-green and scarlet number
for a pair of jeans and crew-neck jumper;
now I'm taller, harder, stronger, older.
Batman, it makes a marvellous picture:
20 you without a shadow, stewing over
chicken giblets in the pressure cooker,
next to nothing in the walk-in larder,
punching the palm of your hand all winter,
you baby, now I'm the real boy wonder.

Mice and snakes don't give me the shivers

Mice and snakes don't give me the shivers,
which I put down squarely to a decent beginning.
Upbringing, I should say, by which I mean
how me and the old man
5 made a good team, and never took
to stepping outside or mixing it up, aside

from the odd time when I had one word too many
for my mother, or that underwater evening
when I came home swimming
10 through a quart of stolen home-brewed damson wine.

So it goes. And anyway, like he says,
on the day I'm broad and bothered and bold enough
to take a swing and try and knock his grin off,

he'll be too old.

Mother, any distance greater than a single span

Mother, any distance greater than a single span
requires a second pair of hands.
You come to help me measure windows, pelmets, doors,
the acres of the walls, the prairies of the floors.

5 You at the zero-end, me with the spool of tape, recording
length, reporting metres, centimetres back to base, then leaving
up the stairs, the line still feeding out, unreeling
years between us. Anchor. Kite.

I space-walk through the empty bedrooms, climb
10 the ladder to the loft, to breaking point, where something
has to give;
two floors below your fingertips still pinch
the last one-hundredth of an inch . . . I reach
towards a hatch that opens on an endless sky
15 to fall or fly.

My father thought it bloody queer

My father thought it bloody queer,
the day I rolled home with a ring of silver in my ear
half hidden by a mop of hair. 'You've lost your head.
If that's how easily you're led
5   you should've had it through your nose instead.'

And even then I hadn't had the nerve to numb
the lobe with ice, then drive a needle through the skin,
then wear a safety-pin. It took a jeweller's gun
to pierce the flesh, and then a friend
10   to thread a sleeper in, and where it slept
the hole became a sore, became a wound, and wept.

At twenty-nine, it comes as no surprise to hear
my own voice breaking like a tear, released like water,
cried from way back in the spiral of the ear. *If I were you,*
15   *I'd take it out and leave it out next year.*

Poem

And if it snowed and snow covered the drive
he took a spade and tossed it to one side.
And always tucked his daughter up at night.
And slippered her the one time that she lied.

5 And every week he tipped up half his wage.
And what he didn't spend each week he saved.
And praised his wife for every meal she made.
And once, for laughing, punched her in the face.

And for his mum he hired a private nurse.
10 And every Sunday taxied her to church.
And he blubbed when she went from bad to worse.
And twice he lifted ten quid from her purse.

Here's how they rated him when they looked back:
sometimes he did this, sometimes he did that.

The Convergence of the Twain

I
Here is an architecture of air.
Where dust has cleared,
nothing stands but free sky, unlimited and sheer.

II
Smoke's dark bruise
has paled, soothed
by wind, dabbed at and eased by rain, exposing the wound.

III
Over the spoil of junk,
rescuers prod and pick,
shout into tangled holes. What answers back is aftershock.

IV
All land lines are down.
Reports of mobile phones
are false. One half-excoriated Apple Mac still quotes the Dow Jones.

V
Shop windows are papered
with faces of the disappeared.
As if they might walk from the ruins – chosen, spared.

VI
With hindsight now we track
the vapour-trail of each flight-path
arcing through blue morning, like a curved thought.

VII
And in retrospect plot
the weird prospect
of a passenger plane beading an office-block.

VIII
But long before dawn,
with those towers drawing
in worth and name to their full height, an opposite was forming,

IX

25   a force

still years and miles off,

yet moving headlong forwards, locked on a collision course.

X

Then time and space

contracted, so whatever distance

30   held those worlds apart thinned to an instant.

XI

During which, cameras framed

moments of grace

before the furious contact wherein earth and heaven fused.

To Poverty

after Laycock

You are near again, and have been there
or thereabouts for years. Pull up a chair.
I'd know that shadow anywhere, that silhouette
without a face, that shape. Well, be my guest.
5 We'll live like sidekicks – hip to hip,
like Siamese twins, joined at the pocket.

I've tried too long to see the back of you.
Last winter when you came down with the flu
I should have split, cut loose, but
10 let you pass the buck, the bug. Bad blood.
It's cold again; come closer to the fire, the light,
and let me make you out.

How have you hurt me, let me count the ways:
the months of Sundays
15 when you left me in the damp, the dark,
the red, or down and out, or out of work.
The weeks on end of bread without butter,
bed without supper.

That time I fell through Schofield's shed
20 and broke both legs,
and Schofield couldn't spare to split
one stick of furniture to make a splint.
Thirteen weeks I sat there till they set.
What can the poor do but wait? And wait.

25 How come you're struck with me? Go see the Queen,
lean on the doctor or the dean,
breathe on the major,
squeeze the mason or the manager,
go down to London, find a novelist at least
30 to bother with, to bleed, to leech.

On second thoughts, stay put.
A person needs to get a person close enough
to stab him in the back.
Robert Frost said that. Besides,
35 I'd rather keep you in the corner of my eye
than wait for you to join me side by side
at every turn, on every street, in every town.
Sit down. I said sit down.

True North

Hitching home for the first time, the last leg
being a bummed ride in a cold guard's van
through the unmanned stations to a platform
iced with snow. It's not much to crow about,

5 the trip from one term at Portsmouth Poly,
all that Falklands business still to come. From there
the village looked stopped; a clutch of houses
in a toy snow-storm with the dust settled

and me ready to stir it, loaded up
10 with a haul of new facts, half expecting
flags or bunting, a ticker-tape welcome,
a fanfare or a civic reception.

In the Old New Inn two men sat locked
in an arm-wrestle – their one combined fist
15 dithered like a compass needle. Later,
after Easter, they would ask me outside

for saying Malvinas in the wrong place
at the wrong time, but that night was Christmas
and the drinks were on them. Christmas! At home
20 I hosted a new game: stretch a tissue

like a snare drum over a brandy glass,
put a penny on, spark up, then take turns
to dimp burning cigs through the diaphragm
before the tissue gives, the penny drops.

25 As the guests yawned their heads off I lectured
about wolves: how they mass on the shoreline
of Bothnia, wait for the weather, then
make the crossing when the Gulf heals over.

Wintering Out

To board six months
at your mother's place, pay
precious little rent
and not lift a finger, don't think
5   for a minute I'm moaning.

It's a doll's house end-terrace
with all the trimmings: hanging baskets,
a double garage,
a rambling garden with
10   a fairy-tale ending and geese

on the river. Inside
it's odd, dovetailed into next door
with the bedrooms
back-to-back, wallpaper walls
15   so their phone calls ring out

loud and clear
and their footsteps on the stairs
run up and down like the practice scales
of a Grade I cornet lesson:
20   their daughter's. From day one

I've been wondering, from the morning
I hoisted the blind
and found
your mother on the lawn
25   in a housecoat and leggings

expertly skewering fallen fruit
with the outside tine
of the garden fork,
then casting it off, overboard
30   into the river. I've said

nothing, held my breath
for a whole season, waited
like Johnny Weismuller
under the ice, held on
35   to surface in a new house, our own

where the wood
will be treated and buffed and the grain
will circle like weather
round the knots
40 of high pressure. Here

we've had to button it: not fly
off the handle or stomp upstairs
yelling *That's it you bastard*
and sulk for a week
45 over nothing. Here

the signs are against us:
some fluke
in the spring water
turning your golden hair lime-green, honey.
50 Even the expert

from Yorkshire Water
taking pH tests
and fur from the kettle
can't put his finger on it.
55 We'll have to go; leave

the bathroom with
no lock, the door that opens
of its own accord, the frostless glass
and pretty curtains
60 that will not meet.

It only takes one night,
your mother
having one of her moments, out
at midnight
65 undercoating the gutter to catch us

in the bath, fooling around
in Cinemascope. Nothing for it but to dip
beneath the bubbles,
take turns to breathe through the tube
70 of the loofah, sit tight

and wait for summer.

Without Photographs

We literally stumble over the bits
and pieces, covered with ash
and tarpaulin, stashed into corners,
all that tackle under the old mill.
5 I don't know how we finally figure it out,
poking around in the half-dark,
coming across the neatly coiled strips
of soft lead-flashing
and the fire-blackened melting equipment,
10 but it all fits together, falls into place.
For three weeks we light up the adapted oil-drum
with anything combustible:
door frames from the tip, spools, bobbins,
pallets, planks, old comics even which we sneak
15 from the house beneath our anoraks
and deliver on the run like parachute drops.

When we are forced to take a few steps backwards
and the heat stays in our faces like sunburn –
that's when the fire is hot enough.
20 We slide the melting-pot across the grill
(a stewing pan with no handle, a cooker shelf)
and toss in the lumps of lead
like fat for frying with. It doesn't melt
like butter, slowly, from the bottom upwards
25 but reaches a point where it gives up its form
the way the sun comes
strongly around the edge of a cloud.
Then it runs, follows the dints
in the pan, covers the base so we see ourselves –
30 an old mirror with patches of the back missing.
For moulds we use bricks.
Like stretcher-bearers we lift the pan
between two sticks then pour the fizzing lead
into the well of a brick.
35 Sometimes it splits it clean in half with the heat.

Today we watch the mould, prod it
through its various stages of setting, and can't wait
to turn it out like a cake, feel
its warm weight and read the brickwork's name
40 cast in mirror writing along its length.
But in the days that come, the shapes will mean less
and less, giving in to the satisfaction of the work.
What there is in the sweat, and the burns,
and the blisters, is unmistakably
45 everlasting. Not what is struck in the forged metal
but in the trouble we know we are taking.

And something about friends, walking home,
grinning like bandits, every pocket
loaded,
50 all of us black-bright and stinking like kippers.

Gillian Clarke

Anorexic

My father's sister,
the one who died
before there was a word for it,
was fussy with her food.
5 'Eat up,' they'd say to me,
ladling a bowl with warning.

What I remember's
how she'd send me to the dairy,
taught me to take cream,
10 the standing gold.
Where the jug dipped
I saw its blue-milk skin
before the surface healed.

Breath held, tongue between teeth,
15 I carried in the cream,
brimmed, level,
parallel, I knew,
with that other, hidden horizon
of the earth's deep
20 ungleaming water-table.

And she, more often than not half-dressed,
stockings, a slip, a Chinese kimono,
would warm the cream, pour it
with crumbled melting cheese
25 over a delicate white cauliflower,
or field mushrooms
steaming in porcelain,

then watch us eat, relishing,
smoking her umpteenth cigarette,
30 glamorous, perfumed, starved,
and going to die.

Baby-sitting

I am sitting in a strange room listening
For the wrong baby. I don't love
This baby. She is sleeping a snuffly
Roseate, bubbling sleep; she is fair;
5 She is a perfectly acceptable child.
I am afraid of her. If she wakes
She will hate me. She will shout
Her hot midnight rage, her nose
Will stream disgustingly and the perfume
10 Of her breath will fail to enchant me.

To her I will represent absolute
Abandonment. For her it will be worse
Than for the lover cold in lonely
Sheets; worse than for the woman who waits
15 A moment to collect her dignity
Beside the bleached bone in the terminal ward.
As she rises sobbing from the monstrous land
Stretching for milk-familiar comforting,
She will find me and between us two
20 It will not come. It will not come.

Clocks

for Cai

We walk the lanes to pick them.
'Ffwff-ffwffs'. He gives them the name
he gives to all flowers. 'Ffwff! Ffwff!'
I teach him to tell the time
5 by dandelion. 'One o' clock. Two.'
He blows me a field of gold
from the palm of his hand
and learns the power of naming.

Coming Home

after teaching a poetry course

A week away and I'm coming home.
At five the car breaks dawn in a surf of balsam,
untangles the hill, the lanes, the B-roads.
Stone towns of northern England stir
5 for the milk and the post.

Bill, his dying wife in his arms a month ago:
Lincolnshire spreads fields of widening gold
about his empty house, sons, daughters,
grandchildren in the sleeping farms,
10 her shadow cooling in the double bed.

The motorway straightens through the eyes of bridges.
Dawn burns off its gasses over Manchester,
and Sarah's broken childhood bleeds again,
her father's love gone sour and retracted to a vice
15 that turns the safe-house dead, and blind, and mute.

South on the M6, sunrise in my mirror
dazzles with tears the distant border country.
Into Wales, and for once I dare drive fast
where the road steps off between mountains into air,
20 Glaslyn blue and silk beyond it.

Jane with her love simpler than marriage
and all pain lost in the simple fact of it,
her body a harp now that the wind stirs.
Tracey, half a mind on poetry, half on visions,
25 still frail as glass from the doctor's silences.

Home through waking villages, Bala yawns and rises.
Llyn Tegid takes a white sail in its palm.
Anne, after lifelong marriage, keeps house alone,
its rooms about her like his shrugged-off coat,
30 rehearses in my mind our house, one day.

The lane narrows and turns between sunburnt fields.
Two hundred miles behind me, you at the door
rising for breakfast, a late dream in your eyes.
The slate's already hot. The bees are in the fuchsia.
35 A rug of sunlight's on the bedroom floor, ours
and the widower's bed spread cool for homecoming.

Cold Knap Lake

We once watched a crowd
pull a drowned child from the lake.
Blue-lipped and dressed in water's long green silk
she lay for dead.

5 Then kneeling on the earth,
    a heroine, her red head bowed,
    her wartime cotton frock soaked,
    my mother gave a stranger's child her breath.
    The crowd stood silent,
10 drawn by the dread of it.

The child breathed, bleating
and rosy in my mother's hands.
My father took her home to a poor house
and watched her thrashed for almost drowning.

15 Was I there?
    Or is that troubled surface something else
    shadowy under the dipped fingers of willows
    where satiny mud blooms in cloudiness
    after the treading, heavy webs of swans
20 as their wings beat and whistle on the air?

All lost things lie under closing water
in that lake with the poor man's daughter.

Hare in July

All spring and summer the bitch has courted the hare,
thrilled to the scent in a gateway, the musk of speed.
Months while I dug and planted and watched a mist
of green grow to a dense foliage,
5 neat rows in a scaffolding of sticks and nets,
nose down, tail up in thickening grass
she has been hunting the hare.

Today the big machines are in the field
raising their cromlechs against the sun.
10 The garden is glamorous with summer.
We cut and rake grass for the fire.
She leaps the bank bearing the weight of her gift,
the golden body of a young jack hare,
blood in its nostrils and a drowning sound.

15 'Drop' we say 'drop'. Heartbeat running out,
its eyes as wide and black as peaty lakes.
I feel under my finger one snapped rib
fine as a needle in a punctured lung
where it leaped too wild against the bitch's jaw.
20 Light fades from its fur, and in its eyes
a sudden fall of snow.

Marged

I think of her sometimes when I lie in bed,
falling asleep in the room I have made in the roof-space
over the old dark parlŵr where she died
alone in winter, ill and penniless.
5 Lighting the lamps, November afternoons,
a reading book, whisky gold in my glass.
At my type-writer tapping under stars
at my new roof-window, radio tunes
and dog for company. Or parking the car
10 where through the mud she called her single cow
up from the field, under the sycamore.
Or looking at the hills she looked at too.
I find her broken crocks, digging her garden.
What else do we share, but being women?

Overheard in County Sligo

I married a man from County Roscommon
and I live in the back of beyond
with a field of cows and a yard of hens
and six white geese on the pond.

5 At my door's a square of yellow corn
caught up by its corners and shaken,
and the road runs down through the open gate
and freedom's there for the taking.

I had thought to work on the Abbey stage
10 or have my name in a book,
to see my thought on the printed page,
or still the crowd with a look.

But I turn to fold the breakfast cloth
and to polish the lustre and brass,
15 to order and dust the tumbled rooms
and find my face in the glass.

I ought to feel I'm a happy woman
for I lie in the lap of the land,
and I married a man from County Roscommon
20 and I live at the back of beyond.

Miracle on St David's Day

'They flash upon that inward eye
Which is the bliss of solitude'
The Daffodils by W. Wordsworth

An afternoon yellow and open-mouthed
with daffodils. The sun treads the path
among cedars and enormous oaks.
It might be a country house, guests strolling,
5 the rumps of gardeners between nursery shrubs.

I am reading poetry to the insane.
An old woman, interrupting, offers
as many buckets of coal as I need.
A beautiful chestnut-haired boy listens
10 entirely absorbed. A schizophrenic

on a good day, they tell me later.
In a cage of first March sun a woman
sits not listening, not seeing, not feeling.
In her neat clothes the woman is absent.
15 A big, mild man is tenderly led

to his chair. He has never spoken.
His labourer's hands on his knees, he rocks
gently to the rhythms of the poems.
I read to their presences, absences,
20 to the big, dumb labouring man as he rocks.

He is suddenly standing, silently,
huge and mild, but I feel afraid. Like slow
movement of spring water or the first bird
of the year in the breaking darkness,
25 the labourer's voice recites 'The Daffodils'.

The nurses are frozen, alert; the patients
seem to listen. He is hoarse but word-perfect.
Outside the daffodils are still as wax,
a thousand, ten thousand, their syllables
30 unspoken, their creams and yellows still.

Forty years ago, in a Valleys school,
the class recited poetry by rote.
Since the dumbness of misery fell
he has remembered there was a music
35 of speech and that once he had something to say.

When he's done, before the applause, we observe
the flowers' silence. A thrush sings
and the daffodils are flame.

My Box

My box is made of golden oak,
my lover's gift to me.
He fitted hinges and a lock
of brass and a bright key.
5 He made it out of winter nights,
sanded and oiled and planed,
engraved inside the heavy lid
in brass, a golden tree.

In my box are twelve black books
10 where I have written down
how we have sanded, oiled and planed,
planted a garden, built a wall,
seen jays and goldcrests, rare red kites,
found the wild heartsease, drilled a well,
15 harvested apples and words and days
and planted a golden tree.

On an open shelf I keep my box.
Its key is in the lock.
I leave it there for you to read,
20 or them, when we are dead,
how everything is slowly made,
how slowly things made me,
a tree, a lover, words, a box,
books and a golden tree.

On the Train

Cradled through England between flooded fields
rocking, rocking the rails, my head-phones on,
the black box of my Walkman on the table.
Hot tea trembles in its plastic cup.
5 I'm thinking of you waking in our bed
thinking of me on the train. Too soon to phone.

The radio speaks in the suburbs, in commuter towns,
in cars unloading children at school gates,
is silenced in dark parkways down the line
10 before locks click and footprints track the frost
and trains slide out of stations in the dawn
dreaming their way towards the blazing bone-ship.

The Vodaphone you are calling
may have been switched off.
15 Please call later. And calling later,
calling later their phones ring in the rubble
and in the rubble of suburban kitchens
the wolves howl into silent telephones.

I phone. No answer. Where are you now?
20 The train moves homeward through the morning.
Tonight I'll be home safe, but talk to me, please.
Pick up the phone. Today I'm tolerant
of mobiles. Let them say it. I'll say it too.
Darling, I'm on the train.

The Angelus

Each note delayed by the swing of the bell,
the slow weight of the rope and a swallowing wind.
Salt air and a fog off the Channel sour with furnacite,
rain on the gate, five elms on a dusk sky.
5 Swiftfoot over the lawn, she left an echo in the trees,
the rope dancing under dripping leaves.

In my room were eight gold counterpanes
that slipped like water when you tried to fold them.
First night, I was alone. They drove away in the rain
10 after family tea at the Seabank, green Lloyd Loom
and Kunzel cakes that tasted of dust,
out-of-season and nobody talking.

My new clothes smelt of navy blue wet wool,
the bloom gone out of them. Night came black to the glass,
15 an oval mirror swam towards me with an open mouth.
Even their kindness and the clean cave of the bed
could not keep me from the tunnel,
the shadows in a hurry along dark corridors.

Years later I went back.
20 They showed me pretty rooms,
bright girls racing somewhere, preoccupied,
and across the lawn where the angelus bell had been
the stumps of five dead elms.

The Field-Mouse

Summer, and the long grass is a snare drum,
The air hums with jets.
Down at the end of the meadow,
far from the radio's terrible news,
5 we cut the hay. All afternoon
its wave breaks before the tractor blade.
Over the hedge our neighbour travels his field
in a cloud of lime, drifting our land
with a chance gift of sweetness.

10 The child comes running through the killed flowers,
his hands a nest of quivering mouse,
its black eyes two sparks burning.
We know it'll die, and ought to finish it off.
It curls in agony big as itself
15 and the star goes out in its eye.
Summer in Europe, the fields hurt,
and the children kneel in long grass
staring at what we have crushed.

Before day's done the field lies bleeding,
20 the dusk garden inhabited by the saved, voles,
frogs, a nest of mice. The wrong that woke
from a rumour of pain won't heal,
and we can't face the newspapers.
All night I dream the children dance in grass,
25 their bones brittle as mouse-ribs, the air
stammering with gunfire, my neighbour turned
stranger, wounding my land with stones.

The Hare

i.m. Frances Horovitz 1938–1983

That March night I remember how we heard
a baby crying in a neighbouring room
but found him sleeping quietly in his cot.

The others went to bed and we sat late
5 talking of children and the men we loved.
You thought you'd like another child. 'Too late.'

you said. And we fell silent, thought a while
of yours with his copper hair and mine,
a grown daughter and sons.

10 Then, that joke we shared, our phases of the moon.
'Sisterly lunacy' I said. You liked
the phrase. It became ours. Different

as earth and air, yet in one trace that week
we towed the calends like boats reining
15 the oceans of the world at the full moon.

Suddenly from the fields we heard again
a baby cry, and standing at the door
listened for minutes, eyes and ears soon used

to the night. It was cold. In the east
20 the river made a breath of shining sound.
The cattle in the field were shadow black.

A cow coughed. Some slept, and some pulled grass.
I could smell blossom from the blackthorn
and see their thorny crowns against the sky.

25 And then again, a sharp cry from the hill.
'A hare' we said together, not speaking
of fox or trap that held it in a lock

of terrible darkness. Both admitted
next day to lying guilty hours awake
30 at the crying of the hare. You told me

of sleeping at last in the jaws of a bad dream.
'I saw all the suffering of the world
in a single moment. Then I heard

a voice say "But this is nothing, nothing
35   to the mental pain".' I couldn't speak of it.
I thought about your dream as you lay ill.

In the last heavy nights before full moon,
when its face seems sorrowful and broken,
I look through binoculars. Its seas flower

40   like cloud over water, it wears its craters
like silver rings. Even in dying you
menstruated as a woman in health

considering to have a child or no.
When they hand me insults or little hurts
45   and I'm on fire with my arguments

at your great distance you can calm me still.
Your dream, my sleeplessness, the cattle
asleep under a full moon,

and out there
50   the dumb and stiffening body of the hare.

Sunday

From the mahogany sideboard in the dining-room
she'd unhook the golden question mark
that unlocked her wedding silver,
slide creamy bone from velvet slots,
5 spoons and forks still powdery with Sylvo,
from their shallow heelprints.

Under the house my father laid his drill,
his ringleted bits, graded and smeared
with a green iridescence of oil.
10 Screwdrivers, hammers, saws, chisels,
a rising scale, tuned and ready.
Sunday was helping day.

Once, alone for a moment, I saw
the bright nails set for striking.
15 With my favourite hammer I rang them home.
Some sank sweetly. Some hung sad heads.
Some lay felled, a toehold in the grain.
He stood like thunder at the door.

In the salt-blind dining-room
20 broken by bells and the silence after,
sprouts steamed sourly in the blue tureen.
The cat mimed at the window.
I levelled myself against the small horizon
of the water jug. The mirrors steadied.

25 If I kept quiet, my eyes on the jug,
tacking across that loop of water,
the day would mend. They'd nap, separately.
The cat would walk the garden at my heel,
and we'd watch the pond an hour, inching
30 a stone to the edge, until it fell.

Wendy Cope

Being Boring

'May you live in interesting times.' – Chinese curse

If you ask me 'What's new?', I have nothing to say
Except that the garden is growing.
I had a slight cold but it's better today.
I'm content with the way things are going.
5 Yes, he is the same as he usually is,
Still eating and sleeping and snoring.
I get on with my work. He gets on with his.
I know this is all very boring.

There was drama enough in my turbulent past:
10 Tears and passion – I've used up a tankful.
No news is good news, and long may it last.
If nothing much happens, I'm thankful.
A happier cabbage you never did see,
My vegetable spirits are soaring.
15 If you're after excitement, steer well clear of me.
I want to go on being boring.

I don't go to parties. Well, what are they for,
If you don't need to find a new lover?
You drink and you listen and drink a bit more
20 And you take the next day to recover.
Someone to stay home with was all my desire
And, now that I've found a safe mooring,
I've just one ambition in life: I aspire
To go on and on being boring.

Engineers' Corner

Why isn't there an Engineers' Corner in Westminster Abbey? In
Britain we've always made more fuss of a ballad than a blueprint
. . . How many schoolchildren dream of becoming great engineers?
Advertisement placed in The Times *by the Engineering Council*

We make more fuss of ballads than of blueprints –
That's why so many poets end up rich,
While engineers scrape by in cheerless garrets.
Who needs a bridge or dam? Who needs a ditch?

5 Whereas the person who can write a sonnet
Has got it made. It's always been the way,
For everybody knows that we need poems
And everybody reads them every day.

Yes, life is hard if you choose engineering –
10 You're sure to need another job as well;
You'll have to plan your projects in the evenings
Instead of going out. It must be hell.

While well-heeled poets ride around in Daimlers,
You'll burn the midnight oil to earn a crust,
15 With no hope of a statue in the Abbey,
With no hope, even, of a modest bust.

No wonder small boys dream of writing couplets
And spurn the bike, the lorry and the train.
There's far too much encouragement for poets –
20 That's why this country's going down the drain.

Exchange of Letters

'Man who is a serious novel would like to hear from a woman who is a poem' – classified advertisement, *New York Review of Books*

Dear Serious Novel,

I am a terse, assured lyric with impeccable rhythmic
flow, some apt and original metaphors, and a music that
is all my own. Some people say I am beautiful.

5 My vital statistics are eighteen lines, divided into three-
line stanzas, with an average of four words per line.

My first husband was a cheap romance; the second was
Wisden's Cricketers' Almanac. Most of the men I meet
nowadays are autobiographies, but a substantial
10 minority are books about photography or trains.

I have always hoped for a relationship with an upmarket
work of fiction. Please write and tell me more about
yourself.

　　　Yours intensely
15　　　　Song of the First Snowdrop

Dear Song of the First Snowdrop,

Many thanks for your letter. You sound like just the kind
of poem I am hoping to find. I've always preferred short,
lyrical women to the kind who go on for page after page.

20 I am an important 150,000-word comment on the
dreams and dilemmas of twentieth-century Man. It took
six years to attain my present weight and stature but all
the twenty-seven publishers I have so far approached
have failed to understand me. I have my share of sex and
25 violence and a very good joke in chapter nine, but to no
avail. I am sustained by the belief that I am ahead of my
time.

Let's meet as soon as possible. I am longing for you to
read me from cover to cover and get to know my every
30 word.

　　　Yours impatiently,
　　　　Death of the Zeitgeist

Strugnell's Sonnets (iv)

Not only marble, but the plastic toys
From cornflake packets will outlive this rhyme:
I can't immortalize you, love – our joys
Will lie unnoticed in the vault of time.
5 When Mrs Thatcher has been cast in bronze
And her administration is a page
In some O-level text-book, when the dons
Have analysed the story of our age,
When travel firms sell tours of outer space
10 And aeroplanes take off without a sound
And Tulse Hill has become a trendy place
And Upper Norwood's on the underground
Your beauty and my name will be forgotten –
My love is true, but all my verse is rotten.

Strugnell's Sonnets (vii)

'At the moment, if you're seen reading poetry in a train,
     the carriage empties instantly.'
   – Andrew Motion in a *Guardian* interview

Indeed 'tis true. I travel here and there
On British Rail a lot. I've often said
That if you haven't got the first-class fare
You really need a book of verse instead.
5 Then, should you find that all the seats are taken,
Brandish your Edward Thomas, Yeats or Pound.
Your fellow-passengers, severely shaken,
Will almost all be loath to stick around.
Recent research in railway sociology
10 Shows it's best to read the stuff aloud:
A few choice bits from Motion's new anthology
And you'll be lonelier than any cloud.
This stratagem's a godsend to recluses
And demonstrates that poetry has its uses.

Lonely Hearts

Can someone make my simple wish come true?
Male biker seeks female for touring fun.
Do you live in North London? Is it you?

Gay vegetarian whose friends are few,
5 I'm into music, Shakespeare and the sun.
Can someone make my simple wish come true?

Executive in search of something new –
Perhaps bisexual woman, arty, young.
Do you live in North London? Is it you?

10 Successful, straight and solvent? I am too –
Attractive Jewish lady with a son.
Can someone make my simple wish come true?

I'm Libran, inexperienced and blue –
Need slim non-smoker, under twenty-one.
15 Do you live in North London? Is it you?

Please write (with photo) to Box 152.
Who knows where it may lead once we've begun?
Can someone make my simple wish come true?
Do you live in North London? Is it you?

Manifesto

I'll work, for there's new purpose in my art –
I'll muster all my talent, all my wit
And write the poems that will win your heart.

Pierced by a rusty allegoric dart,
5 What can I do but make the best of it?
I'll work, for there's new purpose in my art.

You're always on my mind when we're apart –
I can't afford to daydream, so I'll sit
And write the poems that will win your heart.

10 I am no beauty but I'm pretty smart
And I intend to be your favourite –
I'll work, for there's new purpose in my art.

And if some bloodless literary fart
Says that it's all too personal, I'll spit
15 And write the poems that will win your heart.

I feel terrific now I've made a start –
I'll have another book before I quit.
I'll work, for there's new purpose in my art,
And write the poems that will win your heart.

Message

Pick up the phone before it is too late
And dial my number. There's no time to spare –
Love is already turning into hate
And very soon I'll start to look elsewhere.

5 Good, old-fashioned men like you are rare –
You want to get to know me at a rate
That's guaranteed to drive me to despair.
Pick up the phone before it is too late.

Well, wouldn't it be nice to consummate
10 Our friendship while we've still got teeth and hair?
Just bear in mind that you are forty-eight
And dial my number. There's no time to spare.

Another kamikaze love affair?
No chance. This time I'll have to learn to wait
15 But one more day is more than I can bear –
Love is already turning into hate.

Of course, my friends say I exaggerate
And dramatize a lot. That may be fair
But it is no fun being in this state
20 And very soon I'll start to look elsewhere.

I know you like me but I wouldn't dare
Ring you again. Instead I'll concentrate
On sending thought-waves through the London air
And, if they reach you, please don't hesitate –
25 Pick up the phone.

Mr Strugnell

'This was Mr Strugnell's room,' she'll say,
And look down at the lumpy, single bed.
'He stayed here up until he went away
And kept his bicycle out in that shed.

5 'He had a job at Norwood library –
He was a quiet sort who liked to read –
Dick Francis mostly, and some poetry –
He liked John Betjeman very much indeed

'But not Pam Ayres or even Patience Strong –
10 He'd change the subject if I mentioned them,
Or say "It's time for me to run along –
Your taste's too highbrow for me, Mrs M."

'And up he'd go and listen to that jazz.
I don't mind telling you it was a bore –
15 Few things in this house have been tiresome as
The sound of his foot tapping on the floor.

'He didn't seem the sort for being free
With girls or going out and having fun.
He had a funny turn in 'sixty-three
20 And ran round shouting "Yippee! It's begun."

'I don't know what he meant but after that
He had a different look, much more relaxed.
Some nights he'd come in late, too tired to chat,
As if he had been somewhat overtaxed.

25 'And now he's gone. He said he found Tulse Hill
Too stimulating – wanted somewhere dull.
At last he's found a place that fits the bill –
Enjoying perfect boredom up in Hull.'

On Finding an Old Photograph

Yalding, 1912. My father
in an apple orchard, sunlight
patching his stylish bags;

three women dressed in soft,
5 white blouses, skirts that brush the grass;
a child with curly hair.

If they were strangers
it would calm me – half-drugged
by the atmosphere – but it does more –

10 eases a burden
made of all his sadness
and the things I didn't give him.

There he is, happy, and I am unborn.

Reading Scheme

Here is Peter. Here is Jane. They like fun.
Jane has a big doll. Peter has a ball.
Look, Jane, look! Look at the dog! See him run!

Here is Mummy. She has baked a bun.
5 Here is the milkman. He has come to call.
Here is Peter. Here is Jane. They like fun.

Go Peter! Go Jane! Come, milkman, come!
The milkman likes Mummy. She likes them all.
Look, Jane, look! Look at the dog! See him run!

10 Here are the curtains. They shut out the sun.
Let us peep! On tiptoe Jane! You are small!
Here is Peter. Here is Jane. They like fun.

I hear a car, Jane. The milkman looks glum.
Here is Daddy in his car. Daddy is tall.
15 Look, Jane, look! Look at the dog! See him run!

Daddy looks very cross. Has he a gun?
Up milkman! Up milkman! Over the wall!
Here is Peter. Here is Jane. They like fun.
Look, Jane, look! Look at the dog! See him run!

Sonnet of '68

The uproar's over, and the calls to fight
For freedom, the Utopian fantasies.
We took a fairground ride to Paradise
And afterwards there's nothing more, goodnight.

5 The fire burnt out. The veterans, turning grey,
Make legends of the beautiful, wild past.
These will stay with us till we breathe our last:
The red flag and the photograph of Che.

So many speeches. There's a silence now.
10 Each of us walks along the city street
Alone, concerned about his daily bread.

We overreached ourselves a little bit.
Euphoria didn't suit us anyhow.
Those who did not outgrow it – they are dead.

Translated from the German of Harry Oberländer

The Lavatory Attendant

> I counted two and seventy stenches
> All well defined and several stinks!
> Coleridge

Slumped on a chair, his body is an S
That wants to be a minus sign.

His face is overripe Wensleydale
Going blue at the edges.

5 In overalls of sacerdotal white
He guards a row of fonts

With lids like eye-patches. Snapped shut
They are castanets. All day he hears

Short–lived Niagaras, the clank
10 And gurgle of canescent cisterns.

When evening comes he sluices a thin tide
Across sand-coloured lino,

Turns Medusa on her head
And wipes the floor with her.

The Stickleback Song

'Someone should see to the dead stickleback.'
School inspector to London headteacher

A team of inspectors came round here today,
They looked at our school and pronounced it OK.
We've no need to worry, we shan't get the sack,
But someone should see to the dead stickleback,
5 Dead stickleback, dead stickleback,
But someone should see to the dead stickleback.

Well, we've got some gerbils, all thumping their tails,
And we've got a tankful of live water-snails,
But there's one little creature we certainly lack –
10 We haven't a quick or a dead stickleback,
Dead stickleback, dead stickleback,
We haven't a quick or a dead stickleback.

Oh was it a spectre the inspector saw,
The ghost of some poor classroom pet who's no more?
15 And will it be friendly or will it attack?
We're living in fear of the dead stickleback,
Dead stickleback, dead stickleback,
We're living in fear of the dead stickleback.

Or perhaps there's a moral to this little song:
20 Inspectors work hard and their hours are too long.
When they overdo it, their minds start to crack
And they begin seeing the dead stickleback,
Dead stickleback, dead stickleback,
And they begin seeing the dead stickleback.

25 Now all you young teachers, so eager and good,
You won't lose your wits for a few years, touch wood.
But take off as fast as a hare on the track
The day you encounter the dead stickleback.
Dead stickleback, dead stickleback,
30 The day you encounter the dead stickleback.

Tich Miller

Tich Miller wore glasses
with elastoplast-pink frames
and had one foot three sizes larger than the other.

When they picked teams for outdoor games
5 she and I were always the last two
left standing by the wire-mesh fence.

We avoided one another's eyes,
stooping, perhaps, to re-tie a shoelace,
or affecting interest in the flight

10 of some fortunate bird, and pretended
not to hear the urgent conference:
'Have Tubby!' 'No, no, have Tich!'

Usually they chose me, the lesser dud,
and she lolloped, unselected,
15 to the back of the other team.

At eleven we went to different schools.
In time I learned to get my own back,
sneering at hockey-players who couldn't spell.

Tich died when she was twelve.

Carol Ann Duffy

Repetitive - regular 'sestets' → 6 line stanzas
regular metric pattern } love is impossible to
be flawed.

Answer

Permanence of statue
cold, inanimate unfeeling
OR everlasting

Everlasting love

If you were made of stone,
your kiss a fossil sealed up in your lips,
your eyes a sightless marble to my touch,
your grey hands pooling raindrops for the birds,
5 your long legs cold as rivers locked in ice,
if you were stone, if you were made of stone, yes, yes.

expected warmth of
kiss vs cold, lifeless
stone: repulsive

should be sight w/
eyes not marbles →

transferred
epithets

If you were made of fire,
your head a wild Medusa hissing flame,
your tongue a red-hot poker in your throat,
10 your heart a small coal glowing in your chest,
your fingers burning pungent brands on flesh,
if you were fire, if you were made of fire, yes, yes.

disturbing

If you were made of water,
your voice a roaring, foaming waterfall,
15 your arms a whirlpool spinning me around,
your breast a deep, dark lake nursing the drowned,
your mouth an ocean, waves torn from your breath,
if you were water, if you were made of water, yes, yes.

disturbing

If you were made of air,
20 your face empty and infinite as sky,
your words a wind with litter for its nouns,
your movements sudden gusts among the clouds,
your body only breeze against my dress,
if you were air, if you were made of air, yes, yes.

BATHOS: from sublime to everyday

25 If you were made of air, if you were air,
if you were made of water, if you were water,
if you were made of fire, if you were fire,
if you were made of stone, if you were stone,
or if you were none of these, but really death,
30 the answer is yes, yes.

→ till death do us part → marriage

Side and margin annotations:

Works as a riddle?

Implied Question if Poem is the Answer
Will you marry me / Will you love me
after death? etc.

only difference in each stanza is the
element that changes. Repetitive

Either: Declaration of unconditional
love → desperate & will marry
anyone regardless of results

Suggests complete security
of her love ?

Each stanza is a way
of preserving loved
one?

figurative language →
hyperbole, metaphor, simile,
unstoppable /uncontrollable
tone → represents feelings

To put up a statue →
complimentary that
they are loved &
want to be remembered

Natural world

OBSESSIVE LOVE even if the person was all of these awful things, she'd still love them.
Bordering on madness, disturbing. All stanzas magnify to make lover God-like, mythological
character, supernatural → "deep" complimentary, water stanza = complimentary. No idea
that love will be returned → lover may have uncertainty. Effective as a new way of
expressing love
- Suggesting some sort of life long commitment
- Commitment & obsession vs conditional → 'if 's a statement, & will

Refer to the 'speaker' not Duffy

Before You Were Mine

I'm ten years away from the corner you laugh on
with your pals, Maggie McGeeney and Jean Duff.
The three of you bend from the waist, holding
each other, or your knees, and shriek at the pavement.
5 Your polka-dot dress blows round your legs. Marilyn.

I'm not here yet. The thought of me doesn't occur
in the ballroom with the thousand eyes, the fizzy, movie tomorrows
the right walk home could bring. I knew you would dance
like that. Before you were mine, your Ma stands at the close
10 with a hiding for the late one. You reckon it's worth it.

The decade ahead of my loud, possessive yell was the best one, eh?
I remember my hands in those high-heeled red shoes, relics,
and now your ghost clatters toward me over George Square
till I see you, clear as scent, under the tree,
15 with its lights, and whose small bites on your neck, sweetheart?

Cha cha cha! You'd teach me the steps on the way home from Mass,
stamping stars from the wrong pavement. Even then
I wanted the bold girl winking in Portobello, somewhere
in Scotland, before I was born. That glamorous love lasts
20 where you sparkle and waltz and laugh before you were mine.

Brothers

Once, I slept in a bed with these four men who share
an older face and can be made to laugh, even now,
at random quotes from the play we were in. *There's no way
in the creation of God's earth,* I say. They grin and nod.

5 What was possible retreats and shrinks, and in my other eyes
they shrink to an altar boy, a boy practising scales,
a boy playing tennis with a wall, a baby
crying in the night like a new sound flailing for a shape.

Occasionally, when people ask, I enjoy reciting their names.
10 I don't have photographs, but I like to repeat the names.
My mother chose them. I hear her life in the words,
the breeding words, the word that broke her heart.

Much in common, me, with thieves and businessmen,
fathers and UB40s. We have nothing to say of now,
15 but time owns us. How tall they have grown. One day
I shall pay for a box and watch them shoulder it.

[The page contains extensive handwritten annotations surrounding the poem, including:]

Not cold but not affectionate,

deliberately ambiguous

Used as a way to talk 'bout mum

Mum is strong influence in poem

Older than they were - recogniseable but not same

ambiguous - Vvg one occasion - in the past a lot / family resemblance

not really funny... shared family past

If thinks poem's universal when it's not

communication still here but grows apart i deal later stanza

four men who share maybe they are still more connected than CAD

family connection is based on past → good times

Trying to relive past

expectations → dreams of future fade / past dreams of future die - moving

as a girl / identifies them non-complex, ID impression

struggle to form identity / randomly reaching out

→ looking for identity

'bout mum / Duffy has photos of others / lack of sentimentality / metaphor → brother name

Occasionally, when people ask, I enjoy reciting their names.

because her connection to men not bcos she likes names, reciting without emotion

play / can't communicate given emotionally so dif

have → can't communicate themselves

chosen result of breeding, name of her brothers / each bro results in 1 of those

Sarcastic / patronising. / well done / I will, no / doof. / unemployment benefits form

patronising 'family friend may say that! hasn't seen them in a while / distant relation

Much in common, me, with thieves and businessmen

Syntax changes / I have much in common: / it. start to / accentuate irony / on ro - like 'me' / self becomes more significant

One thing left to hold them tog / then nothing in common / they haven't made as much money as her

They don't deserve to shoulder it. They didn't show care for her in life

Gloomy final thought. Next time you meet is that?

carry cross

No wonder bros don't socialise, CAB's fault

CAD: responsible one

'shoulder' the responsibility take burden, mom died bros of them...? now you get to know so

defined by occupation → now you get to know so

family Relationships, past is moving: can't get back
Writing of brothers is vehicle to speak about her mother

Dream of a Lost Friend

You were dead, but we met, dreaming,
before you had died. Your name, twice,
then you turned, pale, unwell. *My dear,*
my dear, must this be? A public building
5 where I've never been, and, on the wall,
an AIDS poster. Your white lips. *Help me.*

We embraced, standing in a long corridor
which harboured a fierce pain neither of us felt yet.
The words you spoke were frenzied prayers
10 to Chemistry: or you laughed, a child-man's laugh,
innocent, hysterical, out of your skull. *It's only*
a dream, I heard myself saying, *only a bad dream.*

Some of our best friends nurture a virus, an idle,
charmed, purposeful enemy, and it dreams
15 they are dead already. In fashionable restaurants,
over the crudités, the healthy imagine a time
when all these careful moments will be dreamed
and dreamed again. *You look well. How do you feel?*

Then, as I slept, you backed away from me, crying
20 and offering a series of dates for lunch, waving.
I missed your funeral, I said, knowing you couldn't hear
at the end of the corridor, thumbs up, acting.
Where there's life ... Awake, alive, for months I think of you
almost hopeful in a bad dream where you were long dead.

Handwritten annotation (top left): Dramatic monologue — 1 speaker, we make our mind up from info from person, like stealing

Handwritten annotation (top right): Duffy used to make a living as writer in school. Making fun of teacher. made out to be caricature → exaggeration of faults. Encapsulates all neg. things she associated with teachers in own time at school into H of Eng. Ridiculing her

Head of English

Handwritten annotation: TITLE — a sense of self importance

Handwritten annotation: pretentious / old fashioned / pompous / narrow minded

Handwritten annotation (left): Patronising / intimidating / demeanouring

Handwritten annotation (right): jealous of having own expertise usurped

Today we have a poet in the class.
A real live poet with a published book.
Notice the inkstained fingers girls. Perhaps

Handwritten annotation: pathetic joke

Handwritten annotation (left): fed up kids / clapping

we're going to witness verse hot from the press.

Handwritten annotation: cliché

5 Who knows. Please show your appreciation
by clapping. Not too loud. Now

Handwritten annotation (left): she thinks the poet is not impressive, stuck in snobbish waste of time

Handwritten annotation: words half rhyme

sit up straight and listen. Remember
the lesson on assonance, for not all poems,
sadly, rhyme these days. Still. Never mind.
10 Whispering's, as always, out of bounds –
but do feel free to raise some questions.
After all, we're paying forty pounds.

Handwritten annotation (right): Rhyme → teacher rhymer ironic & Duffy playing with teacher's prejudice. Duffy is satirising teacher →

Handwritten annotation (left): They wouldn't understand, rude?

Those of you with English Second Language
see me after break. We're fortunate
15 to have this person in our midst.
Season of mists, and so on and so forth.
I've written quite a bit of poetry myself,
am doing Kipling with the Lower Fourth.

Handwritten annotation (right): Her idea of poetry: old, rhyming, complimentuous of any. new, no modern verse

Handwritten annotation: 'To Autumn' poem showing off own knowledge

Handwritten annotation: Richard → associated co. old fashioned

Handwritten annotation (left): Writing about teacher as she thinks is good. Ironic humorous humiliating

Right. That's enough from me. On with the Muse.
20 Open a window at the back. We don't
want winds of change about the place.
Take notes, but don't write reams. Just an essay
on the poet's themes. Fine. Off we go.
Convince us that there's something we don't know.

Handwritten annotation: Mix up of LY Am. presidents

Handwritten annotation (right): source of inspiration. eg. relationships that broke / bathos

Handwritten annotation (right): Unpleasant. Nasty as if she knows ev. & poet doesn't → waste

Handwritten annotation: Teacher shocked by poem

Handwritten annotation (left): Patronising / insultable / disgusting

25 Well. Really. Run along now girls. I'm sure
that gave an insight to an outside view.
Applause will do. Thank you

Handwritten annotation: Insincere

Handwritten annotation (left): wooping in background

very much for coming here today. Lunch
in the hall? Do hang about. Unfortunately
30 I have to dash. Tracey will show you out.

Handwritten annotation (left): not an invitation to stay

Handwritten annotation (bottom):
Egocentric. fixed view on what poetry should be about.
Revenge poem → long lasting
Humiliation   Satirical
Lampooning / ridiculing by making fun of
Blunt.
Portrayal of teacher is entertaining?

Handwritten annotation (bottom right): pretentious person may deserve it.

In Mrs Tilscher's Class

You could travel up the Blue Nile
with your finger, tracing the route
while Mrs Tilscher chanted the scenery.
Tana. Ethiopia. Khartoum. Aswân.
5   That for an hour, then a skittle of milk
and the chalky Pyramids rubbed into dust.
A window opened with a long pole.
The laugh of a bell swung by a running child.

This was better than home. Enthralling books.
10 The classroom glowed like a sweet shop.
Sugar paper. Coloured shapes. Brady and Hindley
faded, like the faint, uneasy smudge of a mistake.
Mrs Tilscher loved you. Some mornings, you found
she'd left a good gold star by your name.
The scent of a pencil slowly, carefully, shaved.
A xylophone's nonsense heard from another form.

Over the Easter term, the inky tadpoles changed
from commas into exclamation marks. Three frogs
hopped in the playground, freed by a dunce,
20 followed by a line of kids, jumping and croaking
away from the lunch queue. A rough boy
told you how you were born. You kicked him, but stared
at your parents, appalled, when you got back home.

That feverish July, the air tasted of electricity.
25 A tangible alarm made you always untidy, hot,
fractious under the heavy, sexy sky. You asked her
how you were born and Mrs Tilscher smiled,
then turned away. Reports were handed out.
You ran through the gates, impatient to be grown,
30 as the sky split open into a thunderstorm.

[Handwritten annotations surround the poem throughout the page]

In Your Mind

The other country, is it anticipated or half-remembered?
Its language is muffled by the rain which falls all afternoon
one autumn in England, and in your mind
you put aside your work and head for the airport
5 with a credit card and a warm coat you will leave
on the plane. The past fades like newsprint in the sun.

You know people there. Their faces are photographs
on the wrong side of your eyes. A beautiful boy
in the bar on the harbour serves you a drink – what?
10 asks you if men could possibly land on the moon.
A moon like an orange drawn by a child No.
Never. You watch it peel itself into the sea.

Sleep. The rasp of carpentry wakes you. On the wall,
a painting lost for thirty years renders the room yours.
15 *Of course*. You go to your job, right at the old hotel, left,
then left again. You love this job. Apt sounds
mark the passing of the hours. Seagulls. Bells. A flute
practising scales. You swap a coin for a fish on the way home.

Then suddenly you are lost but not lost, dawdling
20 on the blue bridge, watching six swans vanish
under your feet. The certainty of place turns on the lights
all over town, turns up the scent on the air. For a moment
you are there, in the other country, knowing its name.
And then a desk. A newspaper. A window. English rain.

Liar

She made things up: for example, that she was really
a man. After she'd taken off her cotton floral
day-frock she was him all right, in her head,
dressed in that heavy herringbone from Oxfam.
5 He was called Susan actually. The eyes in the mirror
knew that, but she could stare them out.

Of course, a job; of course, a humdrum city flat;
of course, the usual friends. Lover? Sometimes.
She lived like you do, a dozen slack rope-ends
10 in each dream hand, tugging uselessly on memory
or hope. Frayed. She told stories. *I lived*
in *Moscow once . . . I nearly drowned . . .* Rotten.
Lightning struck me and I'm here to tell . . . Liar.
Hyperbole, falsehood, fiction, fib were pebbles tossed
15 at the evening's flat pool; her bright eyes
fixed on the ripples. No one believed her.
Our secret films are private affairs, watched
behind the eyes. She spoke in subtitles. Not on.
From bad to worse. The ambulance whinged all the way
20 to the park where she played with the stolen child.
You know the rest. The man in the long white wig
who found her sadly confused. The top psychiatrist
who studied her in gaol, then went back home and did
what he does every night to the Princess of Wales.

[Handwritten annotations surround the poem, including:]

dreams vs reality

holophrastic – 1 word sentence

ambivalent

connotation – 2 diff words joined to make a word/phrase

structured like a story – not harmless childlike things

conversational rapport bringing reader in

Pause separates herself / persona

Brazen – believes what she wants

old fashioned heavy jacket for older men

Mundane contrast of gender

intimidating

1 word sentence, ropes like memories but they are frayed

similes, smile, eyes overpowers, makes herself believe

engaging w. reader

windows to soul makes herself believe

boring life reason for fantasies?

just like me & you

Hoping her life will become something like dreams, not letting go of fantasies

imagery of rope, metaphor – rope doesn't bind, broken

water is calm so lies to make interest

imagery of pebbles

struggling to hold on to past

single word sentence, upsetting

interrogation

Rotten Liar insult were all trying to keep lives going, at diff degrees

Drawing us in to be Susan's audience

lies are not burdening, just tossing them around

lies get bigger & bigger until whole pool/life is taken over by lies

focusing on effect of lies wants us to be interested by her self dramatising

watches intently at how they affect

Tone changes to lecturing

she talks about private affairs out loud tells ppl everything on mind not kept to herself

abduction & murder

abducted a child, harmed them? Because ambulance not police

judge. She thinks he's dressing up playing his part imposed on him by society like Susan

sympathetic friend can't percieve where its heading, judges dressed up person, sharp assertive

Happens broadly commonly

can't blame Susan who psychiatrist himself has fantasies of sex with princess, psych is as bad as patient

distasteful ending

When no one believed her lies she, desperate for attention stole a child (is fantasy?) she has one?

another delusion who is anyone to judge?

how far does she believe her lies

diff bet her & psych is that she says all out loud

Eyes

stanza 2 tells us how Susans like us whereas other stanzas tell us she's diff

"If you give someone enough rope they'll hang themself." Poet didn't do favour by not challenging her Or did she get what she deserved

Mrs Lazarus

— not given age
young - why live
in this way for rest of life?

message: miracle was a cruelty for
everyone, do not mess with natural
cycle, makes reader think - what if
someone came back? welcomed?

· flaws of a man
· mid-Eastern culture
· raw emotion
about bereavement
· resented
sympathetically

fear L never had wife
TRAD. images of relationships

foreshadows the problem of an unfaithful
relationship ripping cloth

I had grieved. I had wept for a night and a day
over my loss, ripped the cloth I was married in
from my breasts, howled, shrieked, clawed
at the burial stones till my hands bled, retched
5 his name over and over again, dead, dead.

Gone home. Gutted the place. Slept in a single cot,
widow, one empty glove, white femur
in the dust, half. Stuffed dark suits
into black bags, shuffled in a dead man's shoes,
10 noosed the double knot of a tie round my bare neck,
gaunt nun in the mirror, touching herself. I learnt
the Stations of Bereavement, the icon of my face
in each bleak frame; but all those months
he was going away from me, dwindling
15 to the shrunk size of a snapshot, going,

going. Till his name was no longer a certain spell
for his face. The last hair on his head
floated out from a book. His scent went from the house.
The will was read. See, he was vanishing
20 to the small zero held by the gold of my ring.

Then he was gone. Then he was legend, language;
my arm on the arm of the schoolteacher – the shock
of a man's strength under the sleeve of his coat –
along the hedgerows. But I was faithful
25 for as long as it took. Until he was memory.

So I could stand that evening in the field
in a shawl of fine air, healed, able
to watch the edge of the moon occur to the sky
and a hare thump from a hedge; then notice
30 the village men running towards me, shouting,

behind them the women and children, barking dogs,
and I knew. I knew by the shrill light
on the blacksmith's face, the sly eyes
of the barmaid, the sudden hands bearing me
35 into the hot tang of the crowd parting before me.
He lived. I saw the horror on his face.
I heard his mother's crazy song. I breathed
his stench; my bridegroom in his rotting shroud,
moist and dishevelled from the grave's slack chew,
40 croaking his cuckold name, disinherited, out of his time.

Disturbing grief
Extreme, emotional
physical grief

Image of
extreme
expected
grief

Image of his
decay

trying to bring
him back to life

suicidal grief / remembrance

coming to terms w.
removing possessions
hard

used to remember
his face

the fact he was less
alive becomes
less imp.

new with sickening
horror → doesn't
want

judgement → how
can she move on?

Biblical image

zombie like image

idea of his
smell = horrified
4th stanza
scent vs
STENCH:
changed views

out of control
rhythmic insane heartbeat

definitive repetition

continued sense of finality.
Alliteration of hard consonant
sense of finality

lost her pair, empty, useless
half a couple

oscillance bet. historical &
modern: biblical & black bags
Time is a healer → he becomes less
of a meaningful person to her
stages of bereavement
Religious imagery icon = rel. portrait
fading grief

anachronistic element
Last element of him left her
no evidence he was ever there

PROCESS OF BEREAVEMENT ready to move on
natural
moved on
New person she's met. forgo how
what intimacy was like

faithful until she stopped grieving
Realised she's moved on →
Happy stanza → 1st part
sense of resolution Ready to

friend of Lazarus
Lazarus- proof of miracle
foreshadowing of Christ's
resurrection   much shorter
in Bible
Playing with time
Biblical story → fictional.
She had every reason to
believe him dead.
was it right to raise
him from dead?
fusing of biblical

knows mrs L to. school
teacher. pleasure in
misfortune

why? morphs to horror

Neither pleased
he's brought
back to life
disgusand
strong en.
to hold
him.
in.

ascended to a man, whose wife has been

heaven &   why faithful   object of ridicule
now
brought back

As if he's brought
back to humiliate himself & wife

Nostalgia

Those early mercenaries, it made them ill —
leaving the mountains, leaving the high, fine air
to go down, down. What they got
was money, dull crude coins clenched
5   in the teeth; strange food, the wrong taste,
stones in the belly; and the wrong sounds,
the wrong smells, the wrong light, every breath –
wrong. They had an ache *here*, Doctor,
they pined, wept, grown men. It was killing them.

10 It was given a name. Hearing tell of it,
there were those who stayed put, fearful
of a sweet pain in the heart; of how it hurt,
in that heavier air, to hear
the music of home – the sad pipes – summoning,
15 in the dwindling light of the plains,
a particular place – where maybe you met a girl,
or searched for a yellow ball in long grass,
found it just as your mother called you in.

But the word was out. Some would never
20 fall in love had they not heard of love.
So the priest stood at the stile with his head
in his hands, crying at the workings of memory
through the colour of leaves, and the schoolteacher
opened a book to the scent of her youth, too late.
25 It was spring when one returned, with his life
in a sack on his back, to find the same street
with the same sign on the inn, the same bell
chiming the hour on the clock, and everything changed.

Stealing

The most unusual thing I ever stole? A snowman.
Midnight. He looked magnificent; a tall, white mute
beneath the winter moon. I wanted him, a mate
with a mind as cold as the slice of ice
5 within my own brain. I started with the head.

Better off dead than giving in, not taking
what you want. He weighed a ton; his torso,
frozen stiff, hugged to my chest, a fierce chill
piercing my gut. Part of the thrill was knowing
10 that children would cry in the morning. Life's tough.

Sometimes I steal things I don't need. I joy-ride cars
to nowhere, break into houses just to have a look.
I'm a mucky ghost, leave a mess, maybe pinch a camera.
I watch my gloved hand twisting the doorknob.
15 A stranger's bedroom. Mirrors. I sigh like this – *Aah.*

It took some time. Reassembled in the yard,
he didn't look the same. I took a run
and booted him. Again. Again. My breath ripped out
in rags. It seems daft now. Then I was standing
20 alone amongst lumps of snow, sick of the world.

Boredom. Mostly I'm so bored I could eat myself.
One time, I stole a guitar and thought I might
learn to play. I nicked a bust of Shakespeare once,
flogged it, but the snowman was strangest.
25 You don't understand a word I'm saying, do you?

Handwritten annotations:

GENDER FREE · where is he being asked q? setting? → court
· The speaker creates sense of showing off being mentally dis
· anxiety to makeup for deprivation
· Girl / Boy? ↳ Idea of wanting small kids to cry may be more disturbing if it was a ...

poetic lang. → unlike persona created. EDUCATED?

friendless & wanted a friend like him? → cry for help

Troubled childhood

Awestruck

→ trying to capture themself as if diff. person DISTURBING self loathing? excluded from norma world sigh of amazement? looking at better material world in awe

→ person giving away a lot.

→ not humorous but frightening – really violence, disturbing behaviour

→ not respectful to person? No one understands
Doesn't realise how much he's giving away. 8

Trying to recreate world he never had but it doesn't work so gets frustrated
Advanced language → someone who would have done well if they chose to be educated. Effortlessly uses elevated lang. frequently

Loneliness → complex person: lonely, excluded could have been something better
· No rhyme dramatic monologue (speaking to himself)
Person caught for crime →

[handwritten annotation across top:] CAD keen on reminiscing about sch days

The Good Teachers

[handwritten annotations surrounding title:] Not of our time · SARCASM · TRIGGERED BY MEMORIES from photo · reliving a memory · SECONDARY SCHOOL Catholic girls sch, formal · TONE = ? ironic / sincere / flattering / genuine? · Found old school photograph · starting pt is photo → A just found pic, brings memories · PAST

You run round the back to be in it again. *→ running to back of queue for school photo mischievous*

No bigger than your thumbs, those virtuous women
size you up from the front row. Soon now,
Miss Ross will take you for double History.
5 You breathe on the glass, making a ghost of her, say
South Sea Bubble Defenestration of Prague.

[annotations:] They are no longer have more authority · teachers in photo shrunk in importance camera · PRESENTING threat of photo from diminished · conversational reader included feature · combat, judging you · PAST · killing? · usually compliment · knowing they're better than you av/lte bel. students · reduces teachers to what they deserve She's sizing them up · Just 2 history topics · Teachers have ownership of subjects as if anyone w. interest is potential enemy, treading on their ground · trading future · talking of herself but includes reader · political Czech

You love Miss Pirie. So much, you are top
of her class. So much, you need two of you
to stare out from the year, serious, passionate.
10 The River's Tale by Rudyard Kipling by heart.
Her kind intelligent green eye. Her cruel blue one.
You are making a poem up for her in your head.

[annotations:] old fashioned imperialistic poetry · learning by rote still but she enjoys lesson so likes it a teacher · diff. personalities not entirely kind · Love poem, crush on her

DARKER SIDE ↓

But not Miss Sheridan. Comment vous appelez.
But not Miss Appleby. Equal to the square
15 of the other two sides. Never, Miss Webb. *Geog.*
Dar es Salaam. Kilimanjaro. Look. The good teachers
swish down the corridor in long, brown skirts,
snobbish and proud and clean and qualified.

[annotations:] Contrast bet. french/Eng teacher · Doesn't like · Business git profession · factual strict lang. · Present? talking 2 Bad Teach. that gd teachers · opinion of themselves, pretentious · Good in eyes of world but not int. · limiting, look up too · unapproachable, antiseptic · locked warmth · better, think they're better bcos they're qualified · virtue untouchable · negative description, arrogance

And they've got your number. You roll the waistband
20 of your skirt over and over, all leg, all
dumb insolence, smoke-rings. You won't pass.
You could do better. But there's the wall you climb
into dancing, lovebites, marriage, the Cheltenham
and Gloucester, today. The day you'll be sorry one day.

[annotations:] "I know what you're up to threat · Refusing to answer question / co operate · Journey through school → running thro' school y7, y10/y11 desperate to leave · Teen alluring world outside of school · building - mortgage society → job there, limited horizons · boring job · teachers say · deterioration of behaviour less respect for teacher · Prison · If she was better at school, she'd have better 1 day, she was sorry. Bittersweet what teacher said was true

---

[bottom notes:]
- Not role models she remembers with affection.
- moves from positive immediate happiness to reminder of
- Teachers unmarried: unusual, successful women would expect to leave job if chose to have family. Expected to be professional tho' not good at teaching. rote learning
- radiate bad memories. → they
- Diminishing exp → reduced to size on photo exhere

War Photographer

In his darkroom he is finally alone
with spools of suffering set out in ordered rows.
The only light is red and softly glows,
as though this were a church and he
5 a priest preparing to intone a Mass.
Belfast. Beirut. Phnom Penh. All flesh is grass.

He has a job to do. Solutions slop in trays
beneath his hands which did not tremble then
though seem to now. Rural England. Home again
10 to ordinary pain which simple weather can dispel,
to fields which don't explode beneath the feet
of running children in a nightmare heat.

Something is happening. A stranger's features
faintly start to twist before his eyes,
15 a half-formed ghost. He remembers the cries
of this man's wife, how he sought approval
without words to do what someone must
and how the blood stained into foreign dust.

A hundred agonies in black-and-white
20 from which his editor will pick out five or six
for Sunday's supplement. The reader's eyeballs prick
with tears between the bath and pre-lunch beers.
From the aeroplane he stares impassively at where
he earns his living and they do not care.

Handwritten annotations throughout the page include:

AO1 language / choices of lang
AO2
Real person, friend of CAD, Sunday magazine — we learn more

Employed by newspaper, provide pics. Target audience might not be pp. More literal. that are caring

weekly, repetition, continues, job. Ever up - lost his job. Violence — who's 2 blame

'S' alliteration — in dry image of stained glass windows. pics are like stained glass windows, distant from him.

redroom where the photos are processed. given time to think about what he's seen. film spooling, pics, showing suffering of war. contrast bet. order in war — do not do it justice. impose order onto chaos

cemetery. solemn religious chant. chapel/church. reciting like a solemn religion. prepares his service but...

Belfast. dead bodies are forgotten & part of ground. not thought much about. Laconic. Impermanence of life. cut like soldiers. Impermanence of life — BIBLE REF.

matter of fact. religious image in bible - human life is forced. feel. unpleasant onomat. Now - green doesn't explode/hurt. Rural England. Home again

Lot of culture references. images & references. Vietnam war picture of Napalm girl 1972. cultural famous pic reference. shows suffering - affects him more than anyone he knew.

As if bringing dead back to life - looks back on photos. back in form of picture. Put to back of mind? Now vividly remember. suppressed memory.

great distress. vital role in war. asks to take picture. remains. wages. death. funeral - "dust to dust". photo - not died in vain for wife. photo taken but has a value for...

A hundred agonies in black-and-white → commercial reality → takes life out of them. reduced to dying for nothing. thus not value. pick most shocking one image. feels responsible for death. leisurely, temporary effect.

temporary exp. → photographer knows this. Even as pics being seen / studied he is on his way to next destination.

Moved from priestly figure then diminished

Brings out suffering of... happens so much, doesn't move us anymore. Become numbed to these things. Not as much effect of pics as he deserves & sufferers deserve.

self doubt - what am I doing it for. not positive about his job - disillusioned - wishes he could do more. pics just for commercial value & do not have effect on public. honest with himself - genuinely affected by sights, not just for money, not cynical. He is more affected than readers. Has matter of fact job to do like a priest.

continuous process - rhymes with diff lengths. continues job.

almost anti war poem - are not remembered if you die. Duffy has admiration for him. What can he do more to wake ppl up 2 suffering. religious symbolism. Photographer = priest, darkroom = cathedral. Like a miracle. someone about to perform miracle: bringing back to life the person.

[handwritten top margin: we learn a lot more about narrator than → insecure, loving, paranoid, overpossessive]

[handwritten top right: maddening quality - have to given what D Duffy thir]

Who Loves You

[handwritten: No '?' in title]

[handwritten: Don't trust ↓]

I worry about you travelling in those mystical machines. *[aeroplanes]*

[hyperbole] Every day people fall from the clouds, dead. *[caesura]*

Breathe in and out and in and out easy. *[safety demonstration - calming themself]*

[incantation repeated words like prayer] Safety, safely, safe home. *[really th first and to advise loved one]*

[Over the top too worried about sunturn so what sh think of something naughty]

[Preserved cool protected inside]

5   Your photograph is in the fridge, smiles when the light comes on.

[hyperbole] All the time people are burnt in the public places. *[execution, being martyred]*

Rest where the cool trees drop to a gentle shade. *[riots, religious intolerance? or sunbum — modern idea]*

Safety, safely, safe home.

[up to date - ???]

[If both stanzas are about sunburn]

Don't lie down on the sands where the hole in the sky is. *[hole in ozone layer: global warming]*

10   Too many people being gnawed to shreds. *[exageration: skin peeling from sunbum]*

Send me your voice however it comes across oceans.

Safety, safely, safe home. *[confusing technology]*

[Danger of night] The loveless men and homeless boys are out there and angry.

Nightly people end their lives in the shortcut. *[dangerous alleyway bringing death upon themselves - didn't take precaution]*

15   Walk in the light, steadily hurry towards me. *[religious]*

Safety, safely, safe home. (Who loves you?) *[protective for good of child]*

Safety, safely, safe home. *[oxymoron]* *[rhetorical q.]*

[like an incantation, chanting] *[knowing when to give freedom]*

[like prayer calming] *[Seems claustrophobic]*

[curiously dated: dated view of past]
[line 1 : fact]
[line 2: people/disasters air disaster, mob]
[line 3 : advice]
[line 4: chant]

[Irregular - no rhyme/rhythm]

[Paranoia, extreme possessiveness - everything]
[overprotective parent.]
[Insecurity in absence of loved ones, intense missing, parody of parent?]
[Irrational fear]
[Persona is not Duffy Probably]

depression

feels v deep about person
living death, heartbreak.
suicidal state

- *Hitch / row in relationship → made up*
- *Turning love to pain, can't help bringing insecurity & unhappiness on themself*
- *Ends on +*
  winter followed by spring

Wintering

around slowing pale wind dragging on

depressed, can't
find joy

All day, slow funerals have ploughed the rain. → *buried / killed off happiness of relationship*
We've done again → *not 1st time rel. failed* *can't get out of miserable mindset*
that trick we have of turning love to pain. *repetition*

things being deceitful *despair, day → night.* *growing worse.* *personification*
Grey fades to black. The stars begin their lies, → *associate w. romance → not reality*
wishes on stars → didn't come true

5 nothing to lose.
I wear a shroud of cold beneath my clothes. → *feels lifeless no matter what.* *romantic irony: shocking & ominous romance = lie*
burial clothing → personification *weapon*

Aggression
'fist'
frustration

Death / lifeless

Night clenches in its fist the moon, a stone. *cold distant lifeless*
I wish it thrown. *violence, hostility* *romantic symbol → just wants thrown away* *romance → held in fist & hurled*
I clutch the small stiff body of my phone. → *hoping partner will call*
desperation

10 Dawn mocks me with a gibberish of birds. → *doesn't view it as optimistic* *noisy disturbing annoyance*
I hear your words, → *goes over argument*
they play inside my head like broken chords. *because she's feeling down EVERYTHING is sad →*

*

→ nothing growing. Nothing coming up.

The garden tenses, lies face down, bereaved,
has wept its leaves.
15 The Latin names of plants blur like belief. → *She used to be passionate 'bout gardening, but now → dispassionate, bleak, dead*

insincerity, disgust

I walk on ice, it grimaces, then breaks. *Ice is personified inanimate things*
All my mistakes *assume hostile persona; everything against*
are frozen in the tight lock of my face. *her*
↘ incapable of loosening features

Bare trees hold out their arms} beseech, entreat,
20 cannot forget. *juxtaposing → they do not comfort*
The clouds sag with the burden of their weight.

The wind screams at the house, bitter, betrayed.
The sky is flayed,
the moon a fingernail, bitten and frayed.

*

25 Another night, the smuggling in of snow.
You come and go, → *he left & came to get his things*
your footprints like a love letter below.
↓
evidence of him being there

[handwritten: Something changes in situation,]

Then something shifts, elsewhere and out of sight, *[handwritten: → heals breach]*

a hidden freight *[handwritten: → not in everyday usage]* *[handwritten: Freight: cargo ship so linked to]*

30 that morning brings in on a tide of light. *[handwritten: Tide – sea etc.]* *[handwritten: → light just shining over horizon.]*

The soil grows hesitant, it blurts in green, *[handwritten: → winter over]*

so what has been

translates to what will be, certain, unseen, *[handwritten: Past is only thing to be sure of]* *[handwritten: repetition cycle of seasons]*

as pain turns back again to love, like this,

35 your flower kiss, *[handwritten: → spring images]* *[handwritten: implies it will go bad again.]*

and winter thaws and melts, cannot resist. *[handwritten: [the f. kiss]]*

[handwritten: → seems as if other person shifted; not aware of her feelings]

[handwritten: some kind of love curse: don't know how last spell lifts, involuntary change from 1 to other 8 both.]

[handwritten: Juxtaposing images of reality vs. romantic imagery]

[handwritten: Pathetic fallacy: nature changes w. sit.]

[handwritten: did no same scenery but sees "differently": short period of time but imagery makes it seem long period of time.]

[handwritten: something short lived made out to be longer?]

[handwritten: Hope at end?]

[handwritten: → cyclical idea = no]

[handwritten: → winter → spring, she's happy = yes]

[handwritten: Our North Country? figurative lang →]

[handwritten: • Title: cold emotionally, pre sy cont. tense: ongoing applied to rel. extended stay warmer]

[handwritten: • regular 3 line stanza (terset) regular meter Iambic pentameter / diameter / pentam]

[handwritten: → regularity of rel. ongoing constant regular break downs, dull mournful.]

[handwritten: • Half rhymes → jarring, discordant effect. Nearly rhyme: awk, wrong like regular coul. relationship, something wrong about love]

[handwritten: • Things being deceitful: lies or "trick" → often seen]

Seamus Heaney

An Advancement of Learning

I took the embankment path
(As always, deferring
The bridge). The river nosed past,
Pliable, oil-skinned, wearing

5 A transfer of gables and sky.
Hunched over the railing,
Well away from the road now, I
Considered the dirty-keeled swans.

Something slobbered curtly, close,
10 Smudging the silence: a rat
Slimed out of the water and
My throat sickened so quickly that

I turned down the path in cold sweat
But God, another was nimbling
15 Up the far bank, tracing its wet
Arcs on the stones. Incredibly then

I established a dreaded
Bridgehead. I turned to stare
With deliberate, thrilled care
20 At my hitherto snubbed rodent.

He clockworked aimlessly a while,
Stopped, back bunched and glistening,
Ears plastered down on his knobbed skull,
Insidiously listening.

25 The tapered tail that followed him,
The raindrop eye, the old snout:
One by one I took all in.
He trained on me. I stared him out

Forgetting how I used to panic
30 When his grey brothers scraped and fed
Behind the hen-coop in our yard,
On ceiling boards above my bed.

This terror, cold, wet-furred, small-clawed,
Retreated up a pipe for sewage.
35 I stared a minute after him.
Then I walked on and crossed the bridge.

Ancestral Photograph

Jaws puff round and solid as a turnip,
Dead eyes are statue's and the upper lip
Bullies the heavy mouth down to a droop.
A bowler suggests the stage Irishman
5 Whose look has two parts scorn, two parts dead pan.
His silver watch chain girds him like a hoop.

My father's uncle, from whom he learnt the trade,
Long fixed in sepia tints, begins to fade
And must come down. Now on the bedroom wall
10 There is a faded patch where he has been—
As if a bandage had been ripped from skin—
Empty plaque to a house's rise and fall.

Twenty years ago I herded cattle
Into pens or held them against a wall
15 Until my father won at arguing
His own price on a crowd of cattlemen
Who handled rumps, groped teats, stood, paused and then
Bought a round of drinks to clinch the bargain.

Uncle and nephew, fifty years ago,
20 Heckled and herded through the fair days too.
This barrel of a man penned in the frame:
I see him with the jaunty hat pushed back
Draw thumbs out of his waistcoat, curtly smack
Hands and sell. Father, I've watched you do the same

25 And watched you sadden when the fairs were stopped.
No room for dealers if the farmers shopped
Like housewives at an auction ring. Your stick
Was parked behind the door and stands there still.
Closing this chapter of our chronicle
30 I take your uncle's portrait to the attic.

A Constable Calls

His bicycle stood at the window-sill,
The rubber cowl of a mud-splasher
Skirting the front mudguard,
Its fat black handlegrips

5 Heating in sunlight, the 'spud'
Of the dynamo gleaming and cocked back,
The pedal treads hanging relieved
Of the boot of the law.

His cap was upside down
10 On the floor, next his chair.
The line of its pressure ran like a bevel
In his slightly sweating hair.

He had unstrapped
The heavy ledger, and my father
15 Was making tillage returns
In acres, roods, and perches.

Arithmetic and fear.
I sat staring at the polished holster
With its buttoned flap, the braid cord
20 Looped into the revolver butt.

'Any other root crops?
Mangolds? Marrowstems? Anything like that?'
'No.' But was there not a line
Of turnips where the seed ran out

25 In the potato field? I assumed
Small guilts and sat
Imagining the black hole in the barracks.
He stood up, shifted the baton-case

Further round on his belt,
30 Closed the domesday book,
Fitted his cap back with two hands,
And looked at me as he said goodbye.

A shadow bobbed in the window.
He was snapping the carrier spring
35 Over the ledger. His boot pushed off
And the bicycle ticked, ticked, ticked.

Blackberry-Picking

For Philip Hobsbaum

Late August, given heavy rain and sun
For a full week, the blackberries would ripen.
At first, just one, a glossy purple clot
Among others, red, green, hard as a knot.
5 You ate that first one and its flesh was sweet
Like thickened wine: summer's blood was in it
Leaving stains upon the tongue and lust for
Picking. Then red ones inked up and that hunger
Sent us out with milk-cans, pea-tins, jam-pots
10 Where briars scratched and wet grass bleached our boots.
Round hayfields, cornfields and potato-drills
We trekked and picked until the cans were full,
Until the tinkling bottom had been covered
With green ones, and on top big dark blobs burned
15 Like a plate of eyes. Our hands were peppered
With thorn pricks, our palms sticky as Bluebeard's.

We hoarded the fresh berries in the byre.
But when the bath was filled we found a fur,
A rat-grey fungus, glutting on our cache.
20 The juice was stinking too. Once off the bush
The fruit fermented, the sweet flesh would turn sour.
I always felt like crying. It wasn't fair
That all the lovely canfuls smelt of rot.
Each year I hoped they'd keep, knew they would not.

Death of a Naturalist

All year the flax-dam festered in the heart
Of the townland; green and heavy headed
Flax had rotted there, weighted down by huge sods.
Daily it sweltered in the punishing sun.
5 Bubbles gargled delicately, bluebottles
Wove a strong gauze of sound around the smell.
There were dragon-flies, spotted butterflies,
But best of all was the warm thick slobber
Of frogspawn that grew like clotted water
10 In the shade of the banks. Here, every spring
I would fill jampotfuls of the jellied
Specks to range on window-sills at home,
On shelves at school, and wait and watch until
The fattening dots burst into nimble-
15 Swimming tadpoles. Miss Walls would tell us how
The daddy frog was called a bullfrog
And how he croaked and how the mammy frog
Laid hundreds of little eggs and this was
Frogspawn. You could tell the weather by frogs too
20 For they were yellow in the sun and brown
In rain.

Then one hot day when fields were rank
With cowdung in the grass the angry frogs
Invaded the flax-dam; I ducked through hedges
25 To a coarse croaking that I had not heard
Before. The air was thick with a bass chorus.
Right down the dam gross-bellied frogs were cocked
On sods; their loose necks pulsed like sails. Some hopped:
The slap and plop were obscene threats. Some sat
30 Poised like mud grenades, their blunt heads farting.
I sickened, turned, and ran. The great slime kings
Were gathered there for vengeance and I knew
That if I dipped my hand the spawn would clutch it.

Digging

Between my finger and my thumb
The squat pen rests; snug as a gun.

Under my window, a clean rasping sound
When the spade sinks into gravelly ground:
5 My father, digging. I look down

Till his straining rump among the flowerbeds
Bends low, comes up twenty years away
Stooping in rhythm through potato drills
Where he was digging.

10 The coarse boot nestled on the lug, the shaft
Against the inside knee was levered firmly.
He rooted out tall tops, buried the bright edge deep
To scatter new potatoes that we picked
Loving their cool hardness in our hands.

15 By God, the old man could handle a spade.
Just like his old man.

My grandfather cut more turf in a day
Than any other man on Toner's bog.
Once I carried him milk in a bottle
20 Corked sloppily with paper. He straightened up
To drink it, then fell to right away
Nicking and slicing neatly, heaving sods
Over his shoulder, going down and down
For the good turf. Digging.

25 The cold smell of potato mould, the squelch and slap
Of soggy peat, the curt cuts of an edge
Through living roots awaken in my head.
But I've no spade to follow men like them.

Between my finger and my thumb
30 The squat pen rests.
I'll dig with it.

Follower

My father worked with a horse-plough,
His shoulders globed like a full sail strung
Between the shafts and the furrow.
The horses strained at his clicking tongue.

5 An expert. He would set the wing
And fit the bright steel-pointed sock.
The sod rolled over without breaking.
At the headrig, with a single pluck

Of reins, the sweating team turned round
10 And back into the land. His eye
Narrowed and angled at the ground,
Mapping the furrow exactly.

I stumbled in his hob-nailed wake,
Fell sometimes on the polished sod;
15 Sometimes he rode me on his back
Dipping and rising to his plod.

I wanted to grow up and plough,
To close one eye, stiffen my arm.
All I ever did was follow
20 In his broad shadow round the farm.

I was a nuisance, tripping, falling,
Yapping always. But today
It is my father who keeps stumbling
Behind me, and will not go away.

Mid-Term Break

I sat all morning in the college sick bay
Counting bells knelling classes to a close.
At two o'clock our neighbours drove me home.

In the porch I met my father crying—
5 He had always taken funerals in his stride—
And Big Jim Evans saying it was a hard blow.

The baby cooed and laughed and rocked the pram
When I came in, and I was embarrassed
By old men standing up to shake my hand

10 And tell me they were 'sorry for my trouble',
Whispers informed strangers I was the eldest,
Away at school, as my mother held my hand

In hers and coughed out angry tearless sighs.
At ten o'clock the ambulance arrived
15 With the corpse, stanched and bandaged by the nurses.

Next morning I went up into the room. Snowdrops
And candles soothed the bedside; I saw him
For the first time in six weeks. Paler now,

Wearing a poppy bruise on his left temple,
20 He lay in the four foot box as in his cot.
No gaudy scars, the bumper knocked him clear.

A four foot box, a foot for every year.

Punishment

I can feel the tug
of the halter at the nape
of her neck, the wind
on her naked front.

5 It blows her nipples
to amber beads,
it shakes the frail rigging
of her ribs.

I can see her drowned
10 body in the bog,
the weighing stone,
the floating rods and boughs.

Under which at first
she was a barked sapling
15 that is dug up
oak-bone, brain-firkin:

her shaved head
like a stubble of black corn,
her blindfold a soiled bandage,
20 her noose a ring

to store
the memories of love.
Little adulteress,
before they punished you

25 you were flaxen-haired,
undernourished, and your
tar-black face was beautiful.
My poor scapegoat,

I almost love you
30 but would have cast, I know,
the stones of silence.
I am the artful voyeur

of your brain's exposed
and darkened combs,
35 your muscles' webbing
and all your numbered bones:

I who have stood dumb
when your betraying sisters,
cauled in tar,
40 wept by the railings,

who would connive
in civilized outrage
yet understand the exact
and tribal, intimate revenge.

Scaffolding

Masons, when they start upon a building,
Are careful to test out the scaffolding;

Make sure that planks won't slip at busy points,
Secure all ladders, tighten bolted joints.

5 And yet all this comes down when the job's done
Showing off walls of sure and solid stone.

So if, my dear, there sometimes seem to be
Old bridges breaking between you and me

Never fear. We may let the scaffolds fall
10 Confident that we have built our wall.

Serenades

The Irish nightingale
Is a sedge-warbler,
A little bird with a big voice
Kicking up a racket all night.

5 Not what you'd expect
From the musical nation.
I haven't even heard one—
Nor an owl, for that matter.

My serenades have been
10 The broken voice of a crow
In a draught or a dream,
The wheeze of bats

Or the ack-ack
Of the tramp corncrake
15 Lost in a no man's land
Between combines and chemicals.

So fill the bottles, love,
Leave them inside their cots.
And if they do wake us, well,
20 So would the sedge-warbler.

Servant Boy

He is wintering out
the back-end of a bad year,
swinging a hurricane-lamp
through some outhouse;

5 a jobber among shadows.
Old work-whore, slave-
blood, who stepped fair-hills
under each bidder's eye

and kept your patience
10 and your counsel, how
you draw me into
your trail. Your trail

broken from haggard to stable,
a straggle of fodder
15 stiffened on snow,
comes first-footing

the back doors of the little
barons: resentful
and impenitent,
20 carrying the warm eggs.

The Early Purges

I was six when I first saw kittens drown.
Dan Taggart pitched them, 'the scraggy wee shits',
Into a bucket; a frail metal sound,

Soft paws scraping like mad. But their tiny din
5 Was soon soused. They were slung on the snout
Of the pump and the water pumped in.

'Sure isn't it better for them now?' Dan said.
Like wet gloves they bobbed and shone till he sluiced
Them out on the dunghill, glossy and dead.

10 Suddenly frightened, for days I sadly hung
Round the yard, watching the three sogged remains
Turn mealy and crisp as old summer dung

Until I forgot them. But the fear came back
When Dan trapped big rats, snared rabbits, shot crows
15 Or, with a sickening tug, pulled old hens' necks.

Still, living displaces false sentiments
And now, when shrill pups are prodded to drown
I just shrug, 'Bloody pups'. It makes sense:

'Prevention of cruelty' talk cuts ice in town
20 Where they consider death unnatural,
But on well-run farms pests have to be kept down.

The Summer of Lost Rachel

Potato crops are flowering,
    Hard green plums appear
On damson trees at your back door
    And every berried briar

5 Is glittering and dripping
    Whenever showers plout down
On flooded hay and flooding drills.
    There's a ring around the moon.

The whole summer was waterlogged
10   Yet everyone is loath
To trust the rain's soft-soaping ways
    And sentiments of growth

Because all confidence in summer's
    Unstinting largesse
15 Broke down last May when we laid you out
    In white, your whited face

Gashed from the accident, but still,
    So absolutely still,
And the setting sun set merciless
20   And every merciful

Register inside us yearned
    To run the film back,
For you to step into the road
    Wheeling your bright-rimmed bike,

25 Safe and sound as usual,
    Across, then down the lane,
The twisted spokes all straightened out,
    The awful skid-marks gone.

But no. So let the downpours flood
30   Our memory's riverbed
Until, in thick-webbed currents,
    The life you might have led

Wavers and tugs dreamily
    As soft-plumed waterweed
35 Which tempts our gaze and quietens it
    And recollects our need.

Wheels within Wheels

I

The first real grip I ever got on things
Was when I learned the art of pedalling
(By hand) a bike turned upside down, and drove
Its back wheel preternaturally fast.
5 I loved the disappearance of the spokes,
The way the space between the hub and rim
Hummed with transparency. If you threw
A potato into it, the hooped air
Spun mush and drizzle back into your face;
10 If you touched it with a straw, the straw frittered.
Something about the way those pedal treads
Worked very palpably at first against you
And then began to sweep your hand ahead
Into a new momentum – that all entered me
15 Like an access of free power, as if belief
Caught up and spun the objects of belief
In an orbit coterminous with longing.

II

But enough was not enough. Who ever saw
The limit in the given anyhow?
20 In fields beyond our house there was a well
('The well' we called it. It was more a hole
With water in it, with small hawthorn trees
On one side, and a muddy, dungy ooze
On the other, all tramped through by cattle).
25 I loved that too. I loved the turbid smell,
The sump-life of the place like old chain oil.
And there, next thing, I brought my bicycle.
I stood its saddle and its handlebars
Into the soft bottom, I touched the tyres
30 To the water's surface, then turned the pedals
Until like a mill-wheel pouring at the treadles
(But here reversed and lashing a mare's tail)
The world-refreshing and immersed back wheel
Spun lace and dirt-suds there before my eyes
35 And showered me in my own regenerate clays.
For weeks I made a nimbus of old glit.
Then the hub jammed, rims rusted, the chain snapped.

III

Nothing rose to the occasion after that
Until, in a circus ring, drumrolled and spotlit,
40 Cowgirls wheeled in, each one immaculate
At the still centre of a lariat.
Perpetuum mobile. Sheer pirouette.
Tumblers. Jongleurs. Ring-a-rosies. *Stet*!

Benjamin Zephaniah

Adultery

We all say we luv honesty
But den wot of de lies we do
Your luv may lie an yet be true,
How honest can you be?

5 Live wid your joyful misery
An madness dat you can't proclaim
How often can you change your name?
How honest can you be?

Fake common norms an decency
10 Designed to give you sleepless nights
Torture your soul an dim your lights,
How honest can you be?

You cannot do conformity
You want to luv more equally
15 But wot of your community,
How honest can you be?

Biko the Greatness

Wickedness tried to kill greatness.
In a corner of South Africa
Where they believed there were
No mothers and fathers
5 No sisters and brothers
And
Where they believed
One could not hear the cries of another,
Wickedness tried to kill greatness.

10 Wickedness tried to build a nation
Of white tyrants.
In a corner of the planet
They arrogantly downpressed
They did not overstand
15 As they suffered the illusion of the God complex,
But these words are not for wickedness.

These words are for greatness,
The greatness that inspired doctors and nurses
To become educated in the art of freedom getting,
20 The greatness that inspired educators to become liberators
And a nation of children to become great themselves.

South Africans in the valley of the shadow of death
Feared no wickedness
Because greatness was at their side
25 And greatness was in their hearts,
When the wind of change went south
Greatness was its trustee, guided by truth.

Now we who witnessed the greatness
Sing and dance to his legacy,
30 We who muse his intelligence
Spread the good news in Reggae, Soul, Marabi

And the theatre of liberation,
Knowing that nobody dies until they're forgotten
We chant Biko today
35 Biko tomorrow
Biko forever.

Wickedness tried to kill greatness
Now wickedness is dead
And greatness lives
40 In Islington
As he lives in Cape Town.

Bought and Sold

Smart big awards and prize money
Is killing off black poetry
It's not censors or dictators that are cutting up our art.
The lure of meeting royalty
5 And touching high society
Is damping creativity and eating at our heart.

The ancestors would turn in graves,
Those poor black folk that once were slaves would wonder
How our souls were sold
10 And check our strategies.
The empire strikes back and waves,
Tamed warriors bow on parades,
When they have done what they've been told
They get their OBEs.

15 Don't take my word, go check the verse
Cause every laureate gets worse,
A family that you cannot fault as muse will mess your mind,
And yeah, you may fatten your purse
And surely they will check you first when subjects need to be
          amused
20 With paid-for prose and rhymes.

Take your prize, now write more,
Faster,
Fuck the truth
Now you're an actor do not fault your benefactor,
25 Write, publish and review,
You look like a dreadlocks Rasta,
You look like a ghetto blaster,
But you can't diss your paymaster
And bite the hand that feeds you.

30 What happened to the verse of fire
Cursing cool the empire?
What happened to the soul rebel that Marley had in mind,
This bloodstained, stolen empire rewards you and you conspire
(Yes Marley said that time will tell)
35 Now look they've gone and joined.

We keep getting this beating,
It's bad history repeating,
It reminds me of those capitalists that say
'Look you have a choice'.
40 It's sick and self-defeating if our dispossessed keep weeping
And we give these awards meaning
But we end up with no voice.

Breakfast in East Timor

Ana Pereira is chewing bloodstained oats
In a home-made home in East Timor.
This morning she woke up to a shower
Of bloodstained rain and the smell of common death.
5 She prayed uncontrollably to a European version of Jesus
Christ, then she went to visit her sister's grave.

She visits her sister's grave every day.

As she was returning home she purchased
An Indonesian newspaper, conceived and printed
10 In Jakarta. Now at her breakfast table
She is trying to understand why her occupiers
Are so interested in the British royal family,
The politics of the European community
And the peace talks in Northern Ireland.
15 She just can't understand why the British royal family
Are not interested in the grave of her sister
Or why Europe is so concerned with money.
She wonders what makes new British Labour so proud
Of its women and a thing called an ethical foreign policy.

20 Ana Pereira has the hands of a man,
Her ears can recognise the sound
Of a loaded Hawk fighter-plane as she sleeps
And her feet are designed to dodge bullets.
You can see her killers in her eyes
25 And an ever present vigilance in her step.
She has carried all her sisters' coffins
On her reinforced shoulders,
She waved all her brothers goodbye
When they graduated to the rank of militants
30 And her distinguished stubbornness envies them,
She too wants to be in the hills.

She wants to know where her father is,
She hates bloodstained oats,
And she would love to visit Europe
35 To see for herself.
For now she will keep remembering,
Negotiating days
Leaving nothing to chance,
Nothing for the Indonesians
40 And nothing for nothing.

Today's breakfast tastes like yesterday's
And today, the death business continues.
Tomorrow she wants so much to be alive.

Chant of a Homesick Nigga

There's too much time in dis dark night,
No civilians to hear me wail,
Just ghosts and rats
And there's no light
5 In dis infernal bloody jail.
I want my Mom
I want my twin
Or any friend that I can kiss,
I know the truth that I live in,
10 Still I don't want to die like dis.

If I had sword and I had shield
I would defend myself no doubt,
But I am weak
I need a meal or barrister to help me out,
15 I know my rights
Now tape dis talk
Of course I am downhearted,
Look sucker I can hardly walk
And the interview ain't even started.

20 You call me nigga, scum and wog
But I won't call you master,
The Home Secretary is not my God,
I trod earth one dread Rasta,
But in dis dumb, unfeeling cell
25 No decent folk can hear me cry
No God fearers or infidel
Can save me from dis Lex Loci.

There's too much time in dis dark night
And all my ribs are bare and bruised,
30 I've never dreamt of being white
But I can't bear being abused,
I'm one more nigga on your boot
Dis night you want dis coon to die,
I have not hidden any loot
35 And you have killed my alibi.

I'm spitting blood,
You're in control,
It's your pleasure to wear me down.
I can't stop thinking
40   You patrol the streets where folk like me are found,
I do recall how I have seen
Your face in school upon a time
Telling the kids how good you've been
And of the joys of fighting crime.

45   I'm hanging on for my dear life,
You give me one more injury,
I've just started to feel like
One more Black Death in custody.
I'd love a doctor or a friend
50   Or any lover I have known,
I see me coming to my end,
Another nigga far from home.

Deep in Luv

The washing of dishes
The feeling out of sight
The very sloppy kisses
The things you do at night,
5 The headache and the heartaches
The other family
The everlasting room mates
The deals over money.
The sight the morning after
10 The breaking of the winds
The down bits and the laughter
The emptying of bins
The feeding of the pussy cat
When pushes come to shove
15 The bills upon the door mat
Dere's more to luv dan luv.

Friends who are too close for comfort
Friends who know too much
In-laws who just have too much front
20 Friends who want to touch,
Dates you must remember
Dates you must forget
Secrets you surrender
Sharing your assets.

25 The snoring and the shaving
A place to squeeze your spots
The childish misbehaving

The birthday you forgot
All of those "I told you so's"
30 All of those "Your rights"
All those "You should change your clothes"
Those lovely pillow fights.
Get the right wallpaper
Make our garden cool
35 Don't disturb the neighbour
Take the kids to school
All those things you promise
The fulfillment thereof
Not wanting to sound sexist
40 Dere's more to luv dan luv.

School days were so different
Now school days are done
Now is all commitments
Must make time for fun
45 Now it's not so physical
Now there's more above
In ways it's kinda spiritual
Dere's more to luv dan luv.

Having a Word

I have learnt that equality
May not mean freedom,
And freedom
May not mean liberation,
5 You can vote my friend
And have no democracy.
Being together dear neighbour
May not mean unity,
Your oppressors may give you chances
10 But no opportunities,
And the state that you are in
May have its state security
Yet you may be stateless
Without protection.

15 You my friend do not have to follow your leader,
The government does not have to govern you,
I'm telling you Mom, you are greater than the law
If you are just when the law is not.
You see, once you are aware that new Labour
20 Does not care for the old workers
You may also know that change
May not mean revolution,
Once you realise that old conservatives
Are running out of things to conserve
25 You may also know that all politicians suck the same.
Babylon must burn,
Burn Babylon, burn.

Politics is like dis,
Life is like dis.
30 Intelligence may not mean intelligent,
The news may not be new.

From where we are
To be awake
May not mean
35 To be conscious.

Jimmy Grows Old

Jimmy's getting old now
He wants softness an romance,
He's checking all dat's movin
He don't want to miss a chance,
5 His rebel style is changing
An he really wants a child,
He really is behaving
Jimmy's no longer wild.

He still has de scars of fights
10 But now it's no fight time,
He don't need de bright lights
An he stays far from crime,
He's lonely in his bedsit
He's given up de scene,
15 De doctor at de clinic said,
"It is part of having been".

He was tough an energetic,
Now where are his friends?
He has none,
20 But he knows so many people who pretend,
De beat is not important
Now he likes a lyrical song,
De doctor at de clinic said,
"You're changing, nothing's wrong".

25 He now sweats in his sleep
He has woke up clutching his pillow,
Each day dressed in underpants
He eyes up his mirror,
Too well known to cry in public,
30 Too weak to be macho,
Feeling like a lifeless object,
Feeling kinda hollow.

Well Jimmy boy said, "What de hell
I might as well get drinking,
35 I did my bit, I did rebel,
Now I am de rebel thinking,
I could write a poem
But I was told dat's sloppy,
All I know is as I grow
40 My strength is getting floppy".

Jimmy's social worker said,
"Jimmy get off the booze"
De parish priest said, "Jimmy
What is de path you choose?"
45 Jimmy said, "I just need friends,
And winters are so cold"
De doctor at de clinic said,
"It's part of growing old".

Press Ups an Sit Ups

Press ups an sit ups an jogging does hurt
But I really mus try to keep fit,
I mus try hard, I mus not eat lard
An I mus put more muscle in it,
5 A session each morning, it never gets boring
After a while it's no hassle,
After sum sweating dere'll be no regretting
Cause den I start putting on muscle.
To get rid of gunge I clean out me lungs
10 By running on one little spot,
Me breathing is deep an I hardly sleep
I get up at 5 on de dot,
I do Tang Sang Doo, a kinda Kung Fu
An I got a wicked left kick,
15 I'm good on de sprint, I drop lots of hints
An I am a real clever dick.

I'd like to do Sumo or something like Judo
But I am stuck doing Shadow Boxing
Well it's a start, it's good fe me heart
20 An it keeps me belly in trim.
It may seem pathetic to be so athletic
When competition is Nil,
When I breath in I fallout, to fallout means sprawl out
An I cannot stand being ill,
25 I puff an pant so I can enhance
De quality of me own life
I wanna be wealthy an if I stay healthy
One day I jus may find a wife,
Press ups an sit ups an jogging does hurt
30 But I really mus try to keep fit,
I wanna live long, I wanna be strong,
I'll spend me life working on it.

Reminders

'The peace garden is opposite the War Memorial,'
Said the old soldier.

'We had to fight to make the peace
Back in the good old days.'

5 'No, the War Memorial is opposite the peace garden,'
Said the old pacifist.

'You've had so many wars to end all wars,
Still millions are dying from the wars you left behind.'

'Look,' said the old soldier.
10 'You chickens stuck your peace garden
In front of our War Memorial to cause non-violent trouble.
This War Memorial is necessary,
It reminds us that people have died for our country.'

'Look,' said the old pacifist,
15 'In the beginning was the peace
And the peace was with God
And the peace was God,
This peace garden is unnecessary but
It reminds us that people want to live for our country.'

Room for Rent

Room for rent, apply within,
So I went in to see,
There was this big tall white man,
He looked afraid of me,
5 I told him I was homeless,
He said the room had gone, so try next door,
If they have not,
Then try number one.

Room for rent, apply within,
10 So I went in to see,
The woman said I must return when Tom comes home
        for tea,
I came back hours later and still Tom was not there,
But I am wise, I am no fool,
I know that Tom don't care.

15 Room for rent, apply within,
So I went in to see,
This man was black, he's just like me,
Yes he should let me be,
He said, "Oh yes, come and sit down",
20 I did just as he said,
I took my hat off to get dread air and he stared at
        my head,
He said "Mate I can't help you, the rumours say
        you're bad",
So rumours make me homeless
And landlords make me mad.

The Woman Has to Die

There is no photo of her smile
Dis female of Baluchistan,
Since when she was a playful child
She took her orders from a man,
5 Her free thinking was deemed as sin
Her intellect and will suppressed,
As church and state wallowed deep in
The twisted faith that they professed.

She would have made a lovely bride
10 But strange love visited her heart,
A strange love from another tribe
He loved her much, him from Kalat,
Ah yes, forbidden love once more
But here the woman has to die,
15 For here the church and state make sure
Nobody dares to question why.

Her own father employed his son
To shoot his sister as she lay,
And then the father cleaned the gun
20 Before they both knelt down to pray,
And now the men can rest assured
That madder men will sing their praises,
Now family honour can be restored
As they misquote Koranic phrases.

25 Damn curse the men and shame on them
Women do not forgive them,
But wish a million deaths to them
These devils are not God's men,
There is no photo of her smile,
30 To make the evil greater
The only photo of dis child
Was her corpse
In the daily paper.

Three Black Males

Three black males get arrested
When they said they seek two whites,
Dis poet said that's expected
For we have no human rights,
5   We die in their police stations
We do nothing to get caught
We are only in white nations
When we win them gold in sports.

Three black males in the system
10   So the system just rolls on.
Can you recognise the victims
When the truth is dead and gone,
Can you recognise their anguish
When they beg you time to care
15   Or do you forget your language
When three black males disappear?

Raphael Rowe is not an angel
And Michael Davis ain't
Let us be straight and factual
20   Randolph Johnson is no saint,
The Home Office has a God complex
But that office is not great
For it does not recognise subtext
Injustice or mistakes.

25   Let all poets now bear witness
Let the storyteller tell
Let us deal with dis white business
Dis democracy's not well,
The cops, the judge and jury
30   Need some helping it does seem
And three black males with a story
Fight
So truth can reign supreme.

What If

If you can keep your money when governments about you
Are losing theirs and blaming it on you,
If you can trust your neighbour when they trust not you
And they be very nosy too;
5 If you can await the warm delights of summer
Then summer comes and goes with sun not seen,
And pay so much for drinking water
Knowing that the water is unclean.

If you seek peace in times of war creation,
10 And you can see that oil merchants are to blame,
If you can meet a pimp or politician,
And treat those two impostors just the same;
If you cannot bear dis-united nations
And you think dis new world order is a trick,
15 If you've ever tried to build good race relations,
And watch bad policing mess your work up quick.

If you can make one heap of all your savings
And risk buying a small house and a plot,
Then sit back and watch the economy inflating
20 Then have to deal with the negative equity you've got;
If you can force your mind and body to continue
When all the social services have gone,
If you struggle on when there is nothing in you,
Except the knowledge that justice cannot be wrong.

25 If you can speak the truth to common people
Or walk with Kings and Queens and live no lie,
If you can see how power can be evil
And know that every censor is a spy;
If you can fill an unforgiving lifetime
30 With years of working hard to make ends meet,
You may not be wealthy but I am sure you will find
That you can hold your head high as you walk the streets.

What Stephen Lawrence Has Taught Us

We know who the killers are,
We have watched them strut before us
As proud as sick Mussolinis.
We have watched them strut before us
5 Compassionless and arrogant,
They paraded before us,
Like angels of death
Protected by the law.

It is now an open secret
10 Black people do not have
Chips on their shoulders,
They just have injustice on their backs
And justice on their minds,
And now we know that the road to liberty
15 Is as long as the road from slavery.

The death of Stephen Lawrence
Has taught us to love each other
And never to take the tedious task
Of waiting for a bus for granted.
20 Watching his parents watching the cover-up
Begs the question
What are the trading standards here?
Why are we paying for a police force
That will not work for us?

25 The death of Stephen Lawrence
Has taught us
That we cannot let the illusion of freedom
Endow us with a false sense of security as we walk the streets,
The whole world can now watch
30 The academics and the super cops
Struggling to define institutionalised racism
As we continue to die in custody
As we continue emptying our pockets on the pavements,
And we continue to ask ourselves
35 Why is it so official
That black people are so often killed
Without killers?

We are not talking about war or revenge
We are not talking about hypothetics or possibilities,
40 We are talking about where we are now
We are talking about how we live now
In dis state
Under dis flag (God Save the Queen),
And God save all those black children who want to grow up
45 And God save all the brothers and sisters
Who like raving,
Because the death of Stephen Lawrence
Has taught us that racism is easy when
You have friends in high places.
50 And friends in high places
Have no use whatsoever
When they are not your friends.

Dear Mr Condon,
Pop out of Teletubby land,
55 And visit reality,
Come to an honest place
And get some advice from your neighbours,
Be enlightened by our community,
Neglect your well-paid ignorance
60 Because
We know who the killers are.

Acknowledgements

We are grateful for permission to reprint the following copyright material:

Simon Armitage: 'About His Person', 'Alaska', 'Gooseberry Season', 'In Our Tenth Year', 'Kid', 'Poem', 'True North', 'Wintering Out' and 'Without Photographs' from *Kid* (Faber, 1992); 'The Hitcher', 'To Poverty', and sonnets 'My father . . .', 'Mother . . .', 'Mice and snakes . . .' from *Book of Matches* (Faber, 1993); and 'The Convergence of the Twain' from *Travelling Songs* (Faber, 2002), all reprinted by permission of Faber and Faber Ltd.

Gillian Clarke: 'Anorexic', 'Baby-sitting', 'Coming Home', 'Cold Knap Lake', 'Hare in July', 'Miracle on St David's Day', 'My Box', 'The Angelus', 'The Hare', 'Marged', 'Overheard in County Sligo', 'Clocks (for Cai)' and 'Sunday' from *Collected Poems* (Carcanet, 1997); 'On the Train' from *Making the Beds for the Dead* (Carcanet, 2004); and 'The Field-Mouse' from *Five Fields* (Carcanet, 1998), all reprinted by permission of Carcanet Press Ltd.

Wendy Cope: 'Engineers' Corner', 'Strugnell's Sonnets iv', 'Strugnell's Sonnets vii', 'Lonely Hearts', 'Mr Strugnell', 'On Finding an Old Photograph', 'Reading Scheme', 'Tich Miller', 'Manifesto', 'The Lavatory Attendant' and 'Message' from *Making Cocoa for Kingsley Amis* (Faber, 1986); 'Being Boring', 'Sonnet of '68' and 'The Stickleback Song' from *If I Don't Know* (Faber, 2001); and 'Exchange of Letters' from *Serious Concerns* (Faber, 1986), all reprinted by permission of Faber and Faber Ltd.

Carol Ann Duffy: 'Stealing' from *Selling Manhattan* (Anvil, 1987), 'War Photographer' and 'Head of English' from *Standing Female Nude* (Anvil, 1985), reprinted by permission of Anvil Press Poetry; 'The Good Teachers', 'Brothers', 'Nostalgia' and 'Before You Were Mine' from *Mean Time* (Anvil, 1993), copyright © Carol Ann Duffy 1993, reprinted by permission of Anvil Press Poetry and Rogers Coleridge & White Ltd; 'In Mrs Tilscher's Class', 'Dream of a Lost Friend', 'In Your Mind', 'Liar' and 'Who Loves You' from *The Other Country* (Anvil, 1990), copyright © Carol Ann Duffy 1990, reprinted by permission of Rogers Coleridge & White Ltd, 20 Powis Mews, London W11 1JN; 'Answer' and 'Wintering' from *Rapture* (Picador, 2005), copyright © Carol Ann Duffy 2005, and 'Mrs Lazarus' from *The World's Wife* (Picador, 2000), copyright © Carol Ann Duffy 2000, reprinted by permission of Pan Macmillan, London.

Seamus Heaney: 'A Constable Calls' and 'Punishment' from *North* (Faber, 2001), 'An Advancement of Learning', 'Ancestral Photograph', 'Blackberry-Picking', 'Death of a Naturalist', 'Digging', 'Follower', 'Mid-Term Break', 'The Early Purges' and 'Scaffolding' from *Death of a Naturalist* (Faber, 1966), 'Wheels within Wheels' from *Seeing Things* (Faber, 2002), 'The Summer of Lost Rachel' from *The Haw Lantern* (Faber, 1987), 'Serenades' and 'Servant Boy' from *Selected Poems 1965–1975* (Faber, 1980), all reprinted by permission of Faber and Faber Ltd.

Benjamin Zephaniah: 'Biko the Greatness', 'Bought and Sold', 'Breakfast in East Timor', 'Chant of a Homesick Nigga', 'Having a Word', 'Reminders', 'The Woman Has to Die', 'Three Black Males', 'What If', 'What Stephen Lawrence has Taught Us' and 'Adultery' from *Too Black Too Strong* (Bloodaxe, 2003), copyright © Benjamin Zephaniah 2003, reprinted by permission of Bloodaxe Books; 'Deep in Luv', 'Press Ups and Sit Ups', 'Jimmy Grows Old' and 'Room for Rent' from *School's Out: Poems Not for School* (AK Press, Edinburgh, 1997), copyright © Benjamin Zephaniah 1997, reprinted by permission of United Agents on behalf of Benjamin Zephaniah.

Robert Browning: The texts of the poems are from *Robert Browning: The Major Works* edited by Adam Roberts, (Oxford World Classics, OUP, 2005).

Geoffrey Chaucer: 'The General Prologue' from *The Canterbury Tales* is from *The Riverside Chaucer* Third Edition, edited by Larry D Benson (Houghton Mifflin Company, 1987).

Thomas Hardy: The texts of the poems are from *The Complete Poems* edited by James Gibson (Palgrave Macmillan, 2001).

Wilfred Owen: The texts of the poems are from *The Poems of Wilfred Owen* edited by Jon Stallworthy (20e, Chatto & Windus, 2006).

Christina Rossetti: The texts of the poems are from *The Complete Poems* edited by R W Crump (Penguin, 2001).

William Shakespeare: The texts of the poems are from *The Complete Sonnets and Poems* edited by Colin Burrow (Oxford World Classics, OUP, 2002).

Every effort has been made to trace and contact all copyright holders before publication. If notified we will be pleased to rectify any errors or omissions at the earliest opportunity.